J. H. Bufford's Lith.

Ephraim Ward

Pastor of the Church from 1771 to 1818.

An Historical Discourse

DELIVERED AT

WEST BROOKFIELD, MASS.,

ON OCCASION OF THE

One Hundred and Fiftieth Anniversary

OF THE

FIRST CHURCH IN BROOKFIELD,

OCTOBER 16, 1867.

BY SAMUEL DUNHAM,

PASTOR OF THE CHURCH.

WITH A POEM AND APPENDIX.

SPRINGFIELD, MASS.:
SAMUEL BOWLES & COMPANY, PRINTERS.
1867.

PRINTERS,
SAMUEL BOWLES & CO.
& BINDERS
SPRINGFIELD MASS.
ELECTROTYPERS.

Prefatory Note.

In the preparation of the following Discourse, the records of Town, Parish, and Church, have been thoroughly explored, and every other available source of information consulted, whether manuscript or printed, monumental or traditionary. Many important biographical and other items have also been obtained by means of a somewhat extensive correspondence.

With the facts, carefully sifted and compared, spread out before him, the author has diligently aimed at impartiality of judgment, accuracy of statement, and exactness in statistics and dates. And it is confidently believed that what he has thus patiently sought, has, to a good degree, been attained.

S. D.

West Brookfield, *November* 5, 1867.

Discourse.

Deuteronomy xxxii. 7.

"REMEMBER THE DAYS OF OLD, CONSIDER THE YEARS OF MANY GENERATIONS; ASK THY FATHER, AND HE WILL SHEW THEE; THY ELDERS, AND THEY WILL TELL THEE."

JUST one hundred and fifty years have passed away since the First Church in Brookfield was founded. We are met here within this house of God to-day to commemorate that event. From the widely diverging paths into which our varied preferences and pursuits have led us, we are gathered once more around the venerable Mother to pay that tribute of respect which is due to her hoary age. And it seems quite in keeping with the object of our assembling, as being well fitted to foster and deepen our reverence, and strengthen the bond of our filial attachment, that we should together recount some of the more important incidents of her long and honorable career. May it not, likewise, fully accord with our own cherished and sacred regard for the past, and prove a source of fresh inspiration and incitement for the future, to "remember the days of old," and "consider the years of many generations;"—thankfully tracing, meanwhile, the finger of God in our history.

Scarcely had the wild Indian ceased to hunt the game of the surrounding forests, and to catch the fish of these neighboring ponds and brooks,—scarcely had the echo of his savage yell died away among these hills, when a Church of Christ was here constituted, and the glad note of the Gospel was sounded forth from the lips of the living preacher. It was at that time the *only* church in all this region of country including a circuit of many miles on either hand.

Of the seventy-three Congregational Churches now in Worcester County, not *one* had then been formed, save the First Church (the Old South) in what is now the City of Worcester, and that was organized only the previous year in 1716. This Church,—a little hardy, brave band of men, fearless of danger, true to Puritan principles, and loyal to Christ, stood absolutely isolated and alone, surrounded only by a broad and desolate waste infested with wild beasts and savages.

The maintenance of the ordinances of religion in the midst of this wilderness, remote from the centres of population, and exposed to the barbarity and cruelty of the sons of the forest, was but in harmony with the devout and heroic spirit and conduct of the Pilgrim Fathers, and early settlers of this Colony, who, for the sake of enjoying their liberty, and of walking according to the faith and order of the Gospel, abandoned the land of their nativity for the rock-bound shores and rugged soil of New England.

From the first settlement of old Quaboag* in 1660, there is reason to believe that God had been publicly worshiped here, with the exception of about a dozen years, from 1675, when the entire town was burned, and the inhabitants dispersed by the Indians, to about the year 1687, when the scattered settlers began again to return.

The fifteen years previous to the dispersion were years of peace and evident prosperity; so that the "several inhabitants of Ipswich" to whom the first grant of land here was

---

* The name was changed to Brookfield on becoming a township in 1673.

made, had grown to a little community of twenty families, who had been enabled to build for themselves a sanctuary in which they might hold public worship on the Sabbath.

Indeed this original grant of the General Court in May 20th, 1660, was made only upon condition that there should be twenty families resident here within three years, and that, within the same time, there should be settled "an able minister," such as the Court should approve; "and that they make due provision in some way or other for the future; either by setting apart of lands, or what else shall be thought meet for the continuance of the ministry amongst them."

From an Historical Address* by Henry A. Sykes, A. M., of Suffield, Connecticut, it appears that Mr. John Younglove, the first minister of that town, "had preached at Quaboag (Brookfield, Massachusetts,) for some time previous to Philip's war," and that after the destruction of this settlement by the Indians in 1675, "he went to Hadley and taught the town or grammar school, till he was invited to Suffield," where he commenced his labors sometime during the year 1679, or early in 1680, and where "he continued until his decease June 3, 1690." Of Mr. Younglove as a minister, "little is known; he was no doubt an educated man, though it is not known that he was a graduate of any college, his name not being among those of the graduates of Harvard, then the only college in America."

There is also an obscure tradition, though no certain evidence, of the existence of an organized church at this early period. We are left much in the dark respecting that portion of our history; for, doubtless, the flames that were kindled

---

* Proceedings on the occasion of the One Hundred and Fiftieth Anniversary of the decease of the Rev. Benjamin Ruggles, at Suffield, Conn., 1859, p. 43.

by the treachery of King Philip's Indians, and which destroyed the town, consumed likewise its most ancient records.

From a petition of the inhabitants of Brookfield to the Honored General Court, assembled at Boston, in November 1698, it appears that for a time previous to that date, they were destitute of the stated ministrations of the Gospel. In that petition* they show "That it is an intolerable burden to continue, as we have done, without the preaching of the word." They further say that they "are not able at present to maintain the worship of God;" that they "are but twelve families"—so slow was the resettlement of the town after the war that drove the first settlers from their chosen home—and that they "are not of estate sufficient to give suitable encouragement to a minister," though, be it said to their credit, they were "*willing to do to the outside of* [*their*] *ability.*"

In answer to their petition it was "ordered that there be twenty pounds paid out of the public Treasury of this Province, towards the support of an orthodox minister for one year to commence from the time of the settlement of such minister amongst them."

According to Mr. Foot's Historical Discourse, tradition relates that Mr. Thomas James, a native of England, minister of Charlestown, Massachusetts, and afterwards a missionary at East Hampton, Long Island, preached the first sermon in this town. "Previously to 1713, a Mr. Smith had been employed here as a minister." In 1715 the records show that Mr. Daniel Elmer, a graduate of Yale College in 1713, in a class of three, had, for a time, been carrying on the work of the ministry, supported in part by the General Court. But in that year he relinquished his labors here, and was succeeded by Mr. Thomas Cheney.

* For the petition in full, see Appendix, Note I.

PASTORS, PASTORATES, AND CONNECTED HISTORY.

But it was not till the third Wednesday in October (the 16th, day) 1717, that this church was formally organized, and Mr. Cheney solemnly ordained its first pastor. The terms of his settlement had been agreed upon about a year and a half before:

"Att a meeting of the Inhabitants of Brookfield, on April ye 5th, 1716; *Voted* y^t Thomas Barnes be moderator for s^d day. *Voted* that Edward Walker, Senr., Joseph Banister, and Elisha Rice, doe further Discourse Mr. Cheney as to his proposals in order to a settlement in s^d Place to carry on ye work of the Ministry."

Mr. Cheney's proposals in his own handwriting were soon obtained, while the people were yet assembled, and "were read in town meeting," in the words following:

"Gentlemen, as to ye Dementions of ye House and Barn you propose to Build for me in case I should settle amongst you, it is my mind and desire with Respect to my House, y^t ye length may be 42 foott, the wedht 20 foott; as to ye stud fourteen foott stud; and as to ye barn, that it may be 30 foott long, and 20 foott wide, w^t a lentow [leanto] on one side.

This from your servant,

Thomas Cheney.

As to ye Glass, Nails and Iron, I will provide and procure myself so far as is necessary to s^d House and Barn.

Thomas Cheney."

Having considered the above proposals,—

"The Inhabitants *Voted firstly*, To Give Mr. Cheney for his salery, fifty-two pounds yearly for three years, and to Rise forty shillings a year untill it comes to seventy pounds, and there to stay.

Secondly, *Voted* y^t Mr. Cheney Have all the Land y^t the Committee Proposed to give Him.

Thirdly, *Voted* To Build him a House and Barn, according to ye Dementions y^t he has given; Mr. Cheney providing Glass, Naills, and Iron.

Fourthly, Voted to Break up, and fence, and fitt to sow Eight acres of Land; four acres upon the Hill; two acres to be planted out with orcharding this year, and four Acres To be Broke up on the plain this year, the other two acres to be done within four years.

Fifthly, Voted to gett Mr. Cheney twenty-five cord of wood yearly his lifetime.

Sixthly, Voted to give Mr. Cheney each man one day's work yearly, for six years, His House and Barn to be built in four years; always Provided Mr. Cheney be our ordained Minister.

THOMAS BARNES, *Moderator*."

The above was "Aproved and alowed by the Committee for Brookfield, May y[e] 16th, 1716, Provided Mr. Cheney be their settled minister three years."

SAMUEL PARTRIDGE,
JOHN PYNCHON,
SAMUEL PORTER,
EBENEZER POMROY, } *Committee for Brookfield.*

As to the amount of land which the Committee proposed to give Mr. Cheney, and which was voted by the town at the above meeting, we find the following record:—

"At a meeting of the Committee for Brookfield March 28, 1716, the Committee taking into consideration a grant made to the first settled minister" [that is the first minister who *should* be settled] "made December 9, 1714 of all y[e] land lying in Brookfield between Mr. Willson's and Mr. Younglove's land, the Committee did this day grant to Mr. Thos. Cheney now minister in s[d] place—all the land aforesaid between s[d] Willson and Younglove's lott, and the 20 acres of meadow belonging to s[d] lott, and also 8 or 10 acres on the plain, and also we grant to him s[d] Cheney 100 acres of land in s[d] place to be taken where he shall chuse —always provided Mr. Cheney become a settled minister in s[d] place. The first grant not to enterfeir upon a grant made for a Highway made November, 1715."

In addition to these several grants the Committee, in the autumn of the same year (October 12, 1716) took the following action:—

"Whereas about 3 years Since the General Court allowed to the Ministry in Brookfield twenty pounds; of which sum Mr. Elmore (Elmer) who left the Ministry there so as he had but one-half part of s^d sum payd to him, there Remayns ten pounds of s^d sum or donation; the Committee Judge it meete this last part be payd to Mr. Thomas Cheney the present minister, as part of his sallery, and have given order to Luke Hitchcock Esq. to get the Money for him."

Provision having thus been made for Mr. Cheney's support, in the following summer (July 16, 1717,) the call was made out, and arrangements made for the ordination:—

"Att a meeting of the Inhabitants of Brookfield by order of the Committee for s^d place Bareing date June ye 28th, 1717.

Voted, That the Reverend Mr. Thomas Cheney shall be ordained minister for the Town.

Voted, The third Wednesday in October next is apointed and sett apartt for Mr. Cheney's ordination.

Voted, That Mr. Tilly Merick and Joseph Banister aQuaint Mr. Cheney with the Town's mind, and as to the day aGreed upon for his ordination, and now made Return y^t Mr. Cheney consents thereto.

Voted, That Tilly Merick, Joseph Banister, Thomas Barnes and Thomas Parsons Doe take care that sutable Provition be made for such Elders and Messengers as may be called to assist in our ordination.

Voted That ye Town Celebrate and Sett apart a Day of fasting and Prayer to Implore God's presents w^t us in this solemn and weighty matter, which day is left to Mr. Cheney to appoint.

Full and clear votes.

Test. THOMAS GILBERT, Moderator."

This action on the part of the town received the hearty sanction of the Committee, and won from them expressions of satisfaction "in the unanimity" of the people "in so Good a work," with the hope that they might "have further ocation to Rejoice in their Good settlement."

The ordination took place as arranged, the Sermon being preached just one hundred and fifty years ago to-day by Rev. Solomon Stoddard* of Northampton, on "The duty of GOS-

---

* Solomon Stoddard was born in Boston; was graduated at Harvard College in 1662, in a class of six; was ordained pastor of the church in Northampton, Massachusetts September 11, 1672; and died February 11, 1729, aged eighty-six. He was grandfather of his colleague and successor, Jonathan Edwards.

PEL MINISTERS to preserve a PEOPLE from CORRUPTION." It was printed.

Mr. Cheney was born at Roxbury* (Massachusetts) in 1690, and was graduated at Harvard College in 1711. He is described as an acceptable preacher, and as sustaining the character of a good man, and a faithful minister. He lived in harmony with this people for a period of more than thirty years, and died December 11, 1747, aged 57.†

But he had lived to see the "Great Awakening" of 1740, and to reap some of the glorious fruits of that stupendous work of Grace. It is a fact which had no equivocal bearing upon the early spiritual life and enlargement of the church that in the autumn of 1740 (October 16,) Whitefield on his way from Leicester to Northampton to see Mr. Edwards, halted here for a night, and, before he left, preached with stirring effect to the inhabitants of this town. It was his second visit to America, and his first preaching tour through New England. And although he was then a young man of less than twenty-six years, and had spent but a few months upon our shores, his fame had spread as if by magic all over the land. Just at that time he was the man about whom more was said and written, good and bad, than about any other man in the country.

It is not strange that the people of this quiet place had a curiosity to see so great a prodigy, and to listen to his far-famed eloquence. They sought to give him a hearing in their little house of worship. But Mr. Cheney shared the common prejudice of the ministers of that day, and, fearing the results of so unusual and irregular a proceeding, would not at first

---

* Sprague's Annals of the American Pulpit, Vol. I. p. 173.

† His grave is at Brookfield (South Parish), a few rods from the entrance at the right.

suffer the meeting-house to be opened. At length, however, so great became the press of the people, he was constrained to yield. But by this time the assembly had become so numerous as to exceed the capacity of the house, and, hence, they withdrew to an open field near at hand, and there with a rock* for his pulpit, and the canopy of heaven for his sounding-board, the youthful preacher poured forth that simple, fervid eloquence of his which fell so sweetly upon the ear, and so mysteriously moved and melted the heart.

As the result of that sermon, by the blessing of God, some sinners were awakened, and there followed a revival in whose labors Mr. Cheney bore an active and efficient part, and the church received a large accession to its membership.

Thus early in our history was the fostering care of a kind Providence made signally manifest, and the first pastor of this ancient church graciously permitted, in the closing years of his life, to see the flock of God materially strengthened, and the borders of this Zion perceptibly enlarged.

The last subject of this revival died in 1819, aged one hundred years and seven months.†

About the time of Mr. Cheney's death, a considerable number of the members of this church were, according to Mr. Foot, dismissed to constitute the church in Western ‡ (Warren).

The people were not long satisfied to be without a settled minister; for, among the loose leaves of the old Town Records, we find, under date October 25, 1748, this vote—"That

---

*The rock on which Mr. Whitefield is supposed to have stood during his sermon is on Foster's Hill, in a field north-west of the late residence of Mr. Baxter Barnes.

† Mercy Banister, widow of Thomas Banister.

‡ Mr. Foot's Historical Discourse on Brookfield, p. 16.

Thursday comforteen night be set apart for fasting and prayer, to God for his Directions with Respect to the setling a Gospel Minister amongst us in this place."

The following month, November 28, the town "voted to concur with the vote of the church in their choice of Mr. Elisha Harding to be their minister." The terms of his settlement as fixed December 22, were as follows:

" *Voted*, That there be given and granted to Mr. Elisha Harding for his encouragement to settle in the Gospel ministry in said town the sum of one thousand pounds old tenor currency.

2*dly*. *Voted*, That there be given and granted to the said Mr. Elisha Harding for his yearly salary and support during the time of his continuance in the ministry aforesaid, the sum of five hundred pounds old tenor currency, accounting the same as though to be paid in Indian corn at 20s. per bushel, and rye at 30s. per bushel, and wheat at 40s. per bushel, and so the five hundred pounds to be diminished or increased yearly in proportion to the prices of those commodities as they shall yearly rise or fall and be commonly bought or sold in said town; provided he release to the town all right to the ministry lands, or, in case he inclines to have the improvement thereof, he have the liberty thereof, allowing and paying as much as any other person or persons would give therefor."

On the 13th day of September, 1749, Mr. Harding was solemnly constituted second pastor. The sermon, entitled "A Monitor for Gospel Ministers,"* was preached by Rev. Nathan Bucknam,† of Medway, from Col. 4: 17, which was published. Mr. Harding was graduated at Harvard College in 1745. He was in College with our honored citizen Jedediah Foster, who was graduated the previous year. He is described as "a gentleman of great benevolence;" as "a man of singular probity and solid learning;" as "one, who *from a*

---

* A copy of this sermon as originally published at Boston in 1749, is the property of James Parker, Esq., of Springfield.

† Rev. Nathan Bucknam was graduated at Harvard College in 1721; was settled minister in Medway over 70 years where he died in 1795 aged 92.

child had known the Holy Scriptures, and made them much the matter of his study." "His public ministrations were serious and adapted to edify and benefit his hearers."

In 1750, March 29,—so rapid had been the growth of the town,—a second parish was incorporated, now known as North Brookfield;* and within its bounds a church was organized May 28, 1752, which took the distinctive name of the "Second Church of Christ in Brookfield," more recently called the "First Church in North Brookfield," of which Rev. Mr. Cushing is the present pastor.

The following year (1753) the people fell into a most unfortunate dispute about the location of a new meeting-house which they proposed to erect. The contention waxed so warm and impetuous at length, as to result in a second sundering of the parish, and the incorporation of the third or South Parish November 8, 1754. A church, with thirty-nine members, was there formed April 15, 1756, known at present as the "Evangelical Congregational Church of Brookfield,"* of which Rev. Mr. Coit is the present pastor. In consequence of the commotion and troubles incident to this last division of the parish, Mr. Harding, at his own request, was dismissed May 8, 1755, having sustained the pastoral office not quite six years.

Two years and a half elapsed, and the third pastor, Mr. Joseph Parsons, was settled. He was a son of Rev. Joseph Parsons of Bradford, Massachusetts, and was graduated at Harvard College in 1752. Among those who were in college at the same time with him, we find, in the class immediately preceding, the name of Eli Forbes, afterwards Dr. Forbes,

---

*North Brookfield was incorporated a town in 1812.

* When the first parish was set off a separate township in 1848, it received the name of West Brookfield, and the third parish retained the original name of Brookfield.

the first pastor of the church in the North Parish, and in the second class that followed him, the name of Nathan Fiske, afterwards Dr. Fiske, the first pastor of the church in the South Parish. These three college mates labored here many years side by side as pastors of the three churches of Brookfield.

Mr. Parsons was ordained November 23, 1757. The gentlemen assisting in his ordination were Rev. Messrs Joseph Parsons of Bradford, David White of Hardwick, Joshua Eaton of Spencer, John Tucker of Newbury, and Isaac Jones of Western (Warren). By the terms of the agreement between him and the parish, he was to receive one hundred and eight pounds lawful silver money as settlement, one half to be paid in one year, and the other half in two years, and a salary of fifty pounds lawful silver money the first and second years, fifty-five pounds the third, and sixty pounds the fourth year until the *eighth* year, when it was to be increased by six pounds, thirteen shillings and four pence, for the remainder of his ministry. Also, from the first, there was to be given him thirty cords of good wood brought to his door annually, to commence when he should begin housekeeping and to continue during his ministry. All this on condition that he should release to the precinct all right and claim to the revenues of the ministry lands.

These so called ministry lands, thus having been alienated from their original intention, were in the following year, December 21, 1758, by a committee appointed and empowered for the purpose, divided among the three precincts or parishes of the town; and, as a final disposition of the portion belonging to the first parish, it was sold, and the interest of the money arising from the sale appropriated towards the support of the minister.

In this same year, it must be noted, there sprung up within the church a serious evil, in the introduction of what was termed *the half-way Covenant;* an evil which, at that period, and in subsequent years, gained considerable currency among the churches of this Commonwealth, as also in other parts of New England. By the civil constitution of Massachusetts in those days, none but church members had a right to vote, or to hold civil offices. As early as 1630 it was ordained "that none but church members should be admitted to the freedom of the body politic."*

The early framers of the Government, in their laudable zeal to establish a Commonwealth upon a solid Christian basis, were led into the error of so mingling the affairs of Church and State as, in the event, to secure, with the blessing of a *religious state*, a more than counterbalancing evil—a *political* and *secular* church. From the first, the government of Massachusetts adopted a *religious* test of citizenship. Hence, as a natural consequence, so strong and universal was the desirė to share the privilege of suffrage, and such was the eagerness of men then as now to enjoy the honors of civil office, that a mighty pressure was brought to bear upon the churches to induce them to receive as members such as had not the proper qualifications for church membership, that is, persons who were wholly ignorant of experimental religion, and who laid no claim to a Christian character. Thus powerfully appealed to, this church, among others, was betrayed into the folly of resorting to the expedient of a form of covenant, by "owning" or assenting to which any person, not of an *immoral* character, who had been baptized in infancy, might be recognized as a

* Barber's Historical Collections of Massachusetts, p. 19.

member, with the privilege of availing himself of the ordinance of Baptism for his children, though not required to partake of the Lord's Supper. This pernicious practice, which prevailed in this church nearly sixty years, during which time about one hundred persons "Owned the Covenant," and were admitted to membership, wrought no little mischief, as we shall have occasion to see at a point farther on in our history.

In 1768 the health of Mr. Parsons had so far declined that he was obliged to suspend preaching; and ere long he was compelled by reason of bodily weakness to abandon his ministerial labors altogether. He lived in feebleness some three years, until January 17, 1771, when he died in the fourteenth year of his ministry, and the thirty-eighth year of his age. His dust sleeps beneath the sod of the Old Burying Ground, over which, since the day of his burial, there have swept the rude blasts of a hundred winters. The spot is marked by a suitable stone, erected, in accordance with a vote of the parish, soon after his decease. Also in the new Cemetery we find another stone sacred to his memory, erected, likewise, by vote of the parish. Upon it we read, "He was an example of patience and resignation, and died strong in faith and full of hope, 'The memory of the just is blessed.'"

Mr. Parsons is said to have been "distinguished for the vivacity of his descriptions, the accuracy of his reasoning, and the persuasiveness of his exhortations." His ministry was eminently a peaceful one. The Records assure us that "the greatest harmony prevailed between him and the people during his life."

The fourth pastor was Rev. Ephraim Ward. He was born at Newton, (Massachusetts,) in 1741, and was graduated at Harvard University in 1763, in a class that produced several men of distinction, among whom was Joshua Upham, a native of Brookfield, who afterwards became Judge of the Supreme Court in the Province of New Brunswick.*

Mr. Ward was ordained here October 23, 1771.† The churches assisting in his ordination were the Second and Third in Brookfield, the churches in Western (Warren), Ware, Spencer, Sturbridge, Newton, Weston, Waltham, and the First Church in Dedham. The sermon on the occasion was preached by Rev. Jason Haven, A. M., pastor of the First Church in Dedham, from I. Thessalonians 5: 12, 13, and was "Printed by Richard Draper in Newbury street," Boston.

The early part of Mr. Ward's pastorate fell upon a dark and stormy period in the history of the country. But, notwithstanding the civil commotions which, during the Revolutionary struggle, disturbed the peace, and threatened the existence, of so many churches, the most uniform and perfect harmony prevailed between him and his people throughout his long and useful ministry. This happy circumstance was probably due, in no small degree, to Mr. Ward himself. For he was a man of an exceeding mild and amiable disposition, and, by his great kindness and affability, he won the high esteem and cordial affection of his people, and, indeed, of all who knew him. "He possessed," says his biographer, "a peculiar talent for cultivating peace. Though he was ready to extend the hand of discipline, when the honor of his Master's cause required it; yet he never resorted to coercive meas-

* He died in London in 1808, while on an official mission to the British Government.

† For the proposed terms of Mr. Ward's settlement, and his reply accepting the same, see Appendix, Note II.

ures till all other expedients to reclaim the delinquent had failed."* Dr. Phelps, who was associated with him in the ministry for a time previous to Mr. Ward's death, makes this comprehensive and significant remark: "*He had no enemies, and all the congregation respected and loved him.*"

As might be expected, Mr. Ward's labors here were not without visible fruits. Although, until near the close of his active labors, there was no year that was specially marked by revival, yet the catalogue shows a steady growth of the church, from year to year, throughout his ministry. Scarcely a year passed, whether in time of war or of peace, but that there were some accessions to the church, and on several different years the number received was such as to indicate a high degree of religious interest in the community. In the year 1775, for instance, *twenty-four* were admitted on profession of faith; in 1776, *nineteen;* in 1780, *thirteen;* in 1806, *nineteen;* in 1807, *fifteen;* in 1808, *eighteen.* In 1814 there occurred a revival of considerable extent and power, though "it was confined principally to that part of the parish called Ragged Hill." During that year *fifty-six* were added to the church upon profession. In the gathering of this precious harvest, however, Mr. Ward was not permitted actively to engage. He had been forced by a partial loss of sight to relinquish his labors for the most part, particularly his public ministrations, in the Fall of 1813; after which "the pulpit was supplied for a considerable time by the aid of the neighboring clergy," until the Summer of 1814, after which several candidates were employed.

On the day of the forty-fifth anniversary of his settlement, October 23, 1816, he had the pleasure of welcoming a colleague, Rev. Mr. Phelps, to whom he might entrust the sa-

* Sketch appended to Rev. Mr. Stone's Funeral Sermon.

cred interests of the church and parish, which had become so greatly endeared to his heart. But he was not suffered long to enjoy this new relation. Little more than a year had passed when he was seized with paralysis, and deprived of the power of utterance. But he soon so far recovered his speech as to be able to furnish abundant assurance of the consolation and joy he felt at the prospect of Heaven; and the following month, February 9, 1818, in the seventy-eighth year of his age, having sustained the pastoral office for nearly half a century, he fell asleep in Jesus. Thus, at the end of one hundred years of our church's history, closed the labors of only its fourth pastor. His funeral sermon was preached by Rev. Micah Stone, pastor of the church in the South Parish, from Hebrews 13: 7 and was entitled, "A Christian People's Remembrance of their Deceased Pastor." It was published. In this discourse Mr. Stone says of Mr. Ward, "As a preacher he was evangelical, plain, and practical. He held a very respectable standing among his brethren in the ministry, and in all the neighboring churches. His apparent sincerity and piety, with the amiable spirit, the sound sentiments, and practical tendency of his discourses, rendered him acceptable and edifying." "A distinguishing excellence of our departed friend was, that he was a minister *out* of the pulpit, as well as in it. He was naturally kind and social in his feelings, and maintained a familiar and friendly intercourse with his people. He readily sympathized with them in their joys and sorrows; and was much disposed to benefit them by his private instructions and prayers. His affability and politeness endeared him to their hearts, and favorably disposed them to religion and its services. Of him we may truly say he

'Allur'd to brighter worlds and led the way.'"

During his ministry the church was strengthened by a total accession of THREE HUNDRED AND SEVENTY-EIGHT MEMBERS.

Among the publications of Mr. Ward is a sermon preached at the funeral of Rev. Nathan Fiske, D. D., 1799; and a sermon from II. Peter 1: 13, delivered on the Thirty-Second Anniversary of his own Ordination, October 23, 1803, and "published at the general request of the hearers." It is noteworthy, as indicating the growth of the population of the parish since that time, and perhaps, also, as showing the present increased rate of mortality, that, during those thirty-two years of his ministry, there were, according to the last named Discourse, but "three hundred and twenty-eight deaths, reckoning several who died in the army in the late Revolutionary War, and including several strangers who died in this place,"—an average of only about *ten* deaths per year, while in these recent years, the average annual mortality has risen to nearly *forty*. It is, moreover, a significant fact that, within the same period of thirty-two years, five hundred and five children were baptized, or an average of nearly *sixteen* annually; whereas, at the present time, not more than *four* or *five* children each year receive this Scriptural Seal;—betraying thus a strange laxity on the part of the church in these days in reference to Infant Baptism, and revealing a wide and unwarrantable departure, in this particular, from the faith and practice of our fathers;—a case which, it is to be regretted, is not without its parallel, in numerous instances, among the professedly pedobaptist churches of the land.

Rev. Eliakim Phelps, the fifth pastor, was born at Belchertown, Massachusetts, March 20, 1790. His parents were Dea. Eliakim and Margaret (Combs) Phelps. He was graduated at Union College, Schenectady, in 1814, where he also pursued his theological studies ; and was licensed to preach by the Consociation of Windham County, Connecticut, September, 1815. He was ordained, as we have already noticed, associate pastor with Mr. Ward, October 23, 1816. The sermon was preached from II. Corinthians 5 : 20, by Rev. Dr. Morse * of Charlestown.

At the time that Mr. Phelps received the call to settle here, the Half-way Covenant was still in force, although it seems to have fallen into disuse two years previously, in 1814. But Mr. Phelps made it a condition of his acceptance of the call that that covenant should be abolished. Accordingly there stands upon the church books this gratifying record, dated August 23, 1816.

" At a meeting of the First Church of Christ in Brookfield, convened by previous notice for the purpose, voted unanimously that the covenant, commonly called the Half-way Covenant, or the covenant allowing the privilege of Baptism to those who entered into it, should be entirely done away. No person in future should be admitted into it ; but, those who have enjoyed it, should be permitted to enjoy it one month from the date hereof."

But, as Dr. Phelps says, "the evil did not end with the *voting* it out." The pernicious effects of the custom became particularly apparent during the great revival which soon attended the labors of Mr. Phelps in 1818. This church, like many others, at that time was composed largely of heads of families, a considerable number of whom came in on the Half-way Covenant plan, without any experience of the renewing

---

* Jedidiah Morse, D. D., known as "the father of American geography," was born at Woodstock, Connecticut in 1761 ; was graduated at Yale College in 1783, and died at New Haven in 1826. Prof. Morse, the inventor of the Telegraph, is his son.

and sanctifying influences of grace in their souls. As a consequence, " when the revival came, there were '*great searchings of heart*' *in* the church as well as *out*." And, "one of the most marked features of that revival," as Dr. Phelps says he has ever considered it, " was the number of conversions *in the church*." This revival, as being the first which occurred in the history of the church, of such manifest power, and so general in its extent, deserves a somewhat particular mention. It should, however, be previously said, as having, doubtless, performed an important part in *preparing the way for* the revival, that the Monthly Concert of prayer had been introduced in 1816; also a meeting for prayer weekly on Wednesday evening, and a third service on the Sabbath. Prior to this time, meetings for prayer, with the exception of small neighborhood meetings, were, for the most part, unknown; they were, at least, an anomaly. Respecting the introduction of the Sabbath evening service, Dr. Phelps says, " The people of Brookfield, when I went among them, were in the habit of observing Saturday evening as holy time, or rather *not* observing Sabbath evening. Their custom was, as they were dressed in their go-to-meeting suit, to spend Sabbath evening in social chat among the neighbors. It was easy to see that whatever of seriousness might have been impressed on their minds by the services of the day, was almost sure to be banished and destroyed by the gossip of the evening. To meet this state of things, I determined to try the effect of a third service for the evening. It worked well. It finally grew into a custom, and for the greater portion of my ministry I had three services on each Sabbath. I think that God owned and blessed the third service quite as evidently as either of the others."

In the Fall of 1817 there were some tokens of a revival,

and six or seven were made hopeful subjects of grace. In the course of the year ten were added to the church. Three years before, also, there occurred, as we have seen, a season, of *special religious interest* with very marked results. But, to quote Dr. Phelps' own words again:

" A revival, in the form and aspects in which it developed itself in 1818, was, to most of the people, a new thing; and it encountered no small degree of opposition. Some of the church-members refused, at first, to let their families attend our meetings. The school-house where we held them was closed against us, and the powers of darkness seemed to be putting forth the utmost of their strength to stop the work. But it was of God, and it went forward. I was myself a mere novice in revivals; and the Holy Spirit, compassionating my weakness, seemed to take the work into his own hands; and a very thorough and delightful work it was It continued in greater or less power for more than a year. Fifty-three were added to the church in one day (December 13, 1818,) and the whole number of conversions, including some who joined other churches, was, probably, not less than one hundred."

Dr. Phelps evidently understates the number; for our catalogue shows an accession to our own membership, during 1818 and 1819, of *one hundred and thirteen*, who may properly be reckoned as the fruits of that work of grace. And during his entire pastorate of ten years there were added in all ONE HUNDRED AND SIXTY-EIGHT, of whom one hundred and forty were on profession.

In the year 1819, April 9, our present Confession of Faith was adopted by a unanimous vote of the church, and ordered to be printed for the use of the members.

The *Covenant* now in use is the same, with the exception of a few unimportant verbal alterations, which was adopted when the church was first organized.*

* The Covenant may be found in the Appendix, Note II.

In 1823 we find Mr. Phelps laboring outside the limits of his own parish, in connection with a revival in the city of Boston; and, at a meeting of this church in August of that year, "it was announced that individuals of Park Street Church, Boston, had presented to the First Church in Brookfield a 'Bible for the Desk,' in consideration of services rendered in the revival, by the pastor of the First Church in Brookfield, whereupon it was unanimously—

Resolved, That the church received with lively sentiments of gratitude this expression of Christian kindness and attachment, and cordially return their thanks for the same."

It was further voted that the pastor be requested to transmit a copy of this resolution to the donors, and also that it be inserted in the Records of the Church.

March 21, 1826, Mr. Phelps proposed a dissolution of his ministerial relation, in order to accept the position of Principal of the Female Classical Seminary which, at that time, and for some years, existed and flourished in this place. This request being granted, he preached his farewell sermon June 18th, although the formal dissolution of the pastoral relation did not take place until the 25th day of October following.

Not long afterwards he accepted an invitation to become Principal of the Female Seminary at Pittsfield. The pastor of the church there being laid aside by sickness, Mr. Phelps was placed in charge of the pulpit. There followed almost immediately an extensive work of grace, during which, it was judged, at least three hundred souls were converted to Christ. Encouraged by this seal of the divine blessing upon his preaching, he was led at once to sunder his connection with the Seminary, and in 1829, he accepted a call to the Presbyterian Church, Geneva, New York, where he had a most successful pastorate of six years, during which time more than four hundred members were added to the church. An attack of cholera in 1834 so far broke down his constitution, and impaired his health, that he was compelled, at length, to relinquish his charge, and retire from the active duties of the ministry. In the autumn of the following year he was elected Corresponding Secretary of the American Education Society for the Southern field, with his residence in Philadelphia; the duties of which office he continued to discharge till 1847, and the next year removed to Stratford, Connecticut, where he hoped to spend his days in retirement. But less than three years afterwards, he returned to Philadelphia, where he continued, preaching, much of the time, for some years, though without a charge. At present he is residing with one of his sons in Jersey City, New Jersey, where he enjoys "good health" and "great comfort and peace of mind" in the seventy-eighth year of his age. The degree of Doctor of Divinity was conferred upon him in 1842 by his own Alma Mater.

The publications of Dr. Phelps are, a Sermon preached at the funeral of Judge Dwight Foster in Brookfield, 1823; an Oration delivered on the 4th of July at Geneva, New York, 1832; a Tract entitled "Lydia Sturtevant, or The Fatal Resolution," 1833;* three Adresses, delivered respectively at New York, Boston, and Detroit; and a number of articles in the Philadelphia Observer of whose editorial department Dr. Phelps had charge for about two years.

The same day on which Mr. Phelps was dismissed, (Octo-

---

*A prize tract, one of ten to which prizes of $50 each were awarded out of more than five hundred competitors. It had a sale of 140,000 within the first six months. It is a true narrative of a case that occurred in Brookfield during his ministry here.

ber 25, 1826,) the sixth pastor, Rev. Joseph I. Foot was ordained. Mr. Foot was born November 17, 1796, at Watertown, Connecticut; was graduated at Union College in 1821, and studied theology at Andover Seminary. At his ordination Rev. Thomas Snell, D. D. of North Brookfield made the introductory prayer; the sermon was preached from I. Corinthians 3 : 6, by Rev. Heman Humphrey, D. D., President of Amherst College; consecrating prayer, by Rev. Micah Stone of Brookfield, South Parish; charge to the pastor, by Rev. Timothy M. Cooley, D. D. of Granville; right hand of fellowship, by Rev. Munson Gaylord of Western (Warren); charge to the people, by Rev. John Fiske of New Braintree; and concluding prayer, by Rev. Eliakim Phelps, former pastor.

A powerful work of grace soon followed the labors of the new pastor, and the year 1827 is one of the memorable revival years in our history. During that year *seventy-six* were admitted to the church on profession of faith.

After a pastorate of five and a half years, in which time ONE HUNDRED AND TWENTY-TWO were added to the church, of whom twenty-five united by letter, Mr. Foot was dismissed, at his own request, May 1, 1832.

The following year he assumed the charge of the church in Salina, New York, where he labored two years. In 1835 he accepted a call from the church in Cortland in the same state, and continued his labors there till 1837. He accepted an invitation to the pastorate of the church in Knoxville, Tennessee, in 1839; and, two months afterward, was chosen President of Washington College in that state. In the following March he received from the College the degree of Doctor of Divinity. "On Monday, the 20th of April, 1840, as he was riding to Washington College to be inaugurated president, his horse took fright as he was descending a hill, and he was violently thrown against a rock; by which occurrence three of his ribs were broken, and his lungs pierced by the splinters. He lingered in great distress for twenty-two hours. On the next day, at 4 o'clock, P. M., the day before his expected inauguration, he expired in the forty-fourth year of his age."

Mr. Foot's "Historical Discourse on Brookfield," delivered on the day of the annual Thanksgiving, November 27, 1828, and subsequently published with a valuable Appendix of forty-eight pages, is a lasting monument of his faithful research, and a rare acquisition to the annals of this ancient town.

The seventh pastor was Rev. Francis Horton. He was born in Boston, November 29, 1803; prepared for college chiefly under the instruction of Rev. Enoch Pond of Ward, now better known as Dr. Pond, Professor at Bangor, (Me.) Theological Seminary, and was graduated at Brown University in 1828. He studied theology with Rev. S. Holmes of New Bedford; was approbated to preach by the Old Colony Association, and ordained December 2, 1829, at Dartmouth, Massachusetts, where he labored in the ministry about two years. He was installed pastor of this church August 15, 1832, three months and a half from the day of Mr. Foot's dismission. The Council met for the examination of the candidate the previous evening, and organized by the choice of Rev. John Fiske of New Braintree, moderator, and Rev. Joseph S. Clark of Sturbridge, scribe. The installation services occurred the next day in the forenoon, a prayer-meeting having been held the same morning at sunrise, with reference to the occasion. The parts performed were as follows: prayer by Rev. Augustus B. Reed of Ware, First Church; sermon by Rev. Thomas Snell, D. D. of North Brookfield; installing prayer by Rev. John Fiske of New Braintree; charge to the pastor by Rev. Joseph Vaill of Brimfield; right hand of fellowship by Rev. John Wilder of Charlton; charge to the people by Rev. Micah Stone of Brookfield, South Parish; concluding prayer by Rev. Charles Fitch of Western (now Warren). Other churches represented in the Council were Ware (East) and Millbury.

The relation thus happily formed continued for nine years and one month, when by mutual council, at Mr. Horton's own request, it was dissolved September 15, 1841. The winter following he spent at the South, for the benefit of his health.

In 1843 he was elected pastor of the Orthodox Congregational Church in West Cambridge, and retired from that office in 1854. Early in the year 1856, he received a call to the pastoral care of the church in Barrington, Rhode Island, which was duly accepted; and there his labors are still continued. He has published "A Biography of Jane Bailey," and "Fire-Side Lectures for Sabbath Evenings."

During the ministry of Mr. Horton here, the church was greatly blessed and strengthened. ONE HUNDRED AND NINETY were added to the church, of whom one hundred and forty were received on profession of faith. Two seasons of deep and special religious interest were enjoyed,—in 1835 and 1839. But the year 1835 deserves especially to be commemorated as one of "the years of the right hand of the Most High," when God poured out his Spirit mightily, and graciously turned the feet of many into the way of life. In that one year, eighty-nine made a public profession of their faith, and united with the church. This seems to have been a *culminating point* in the prosperity and growth of the church. The largest membership that the church has ever had was at the close of the year 1835, after all the sheaves of that precious harvest had been gathered in. There were, at that time, three hundred and eighty-one members. By frequent "times of refreshing from the presence of the Lord" the church, for many years, previously, had been very perceptibly increasing in numbers, beyond all the annual losses from deaths and removals. For instance, Mr. Phelps found the church in 1816 with two hundred and thirty-six members; saw that number swelled to three hundred and forty within three years; and left the church in 1826 with a membership of two hundred and ninety, — a total gain, during his pastorate, of fifty-four. Mr. Foot immediately took the church with two hundred and ninety members; saw it increased within two years to three hundred and sixty-six; and left it in 1832 with a membership of three hundred and forty-two, — a gain, during his entire pastorate, of fifty-two. Mr. Horton found the church with three hundred and thirty-six members; and was permitted, in a little more than three years, to see the number rise to three hundred and eighty-one. But from that time, notwithstanding the revival of 1839 brought an accession of twenty-nine members, the yearly losses more than balance the gains, so that Mr. Horton left the church in 1841 with a membership of three hundred and forty-five, — a total gain of only nine, or one member for each year of his pastorate; although it should be said that the average yearly losses by death and ordinary dismission, during those nine years, were very unusually great.

From the year 1835 onwards, the records show a gradual

decrease in the membership of the church for a period of nearly thirty years;* though not all of those years, by any means, were without some cheering tokens of the divine blessing. The cause of this lapse into spiritual coldness, and of this long decline will soon appear.

Four months after the dismission of Mr. Horton, January 12, 1842, the eighth pastor was settled, Rev. Moses Chase. The brief period of Mr. Chase's pastorate forms a black chapter in the history of this church, the particulars of which it would neither be pleasant nor profitable to recall. Suffice it to say that the troubles and distresses of that most unhappy period grew out of the fierce antagonisms that were engendered by the new anti-slavery movements of the time. The conservative wing of the church, headed by a strong-willed, disputatious, and not over discreet pastor, arrayed against a less number of earnest, determined, and somewhat excited radicals, will indicate, in a word, the painful attitude of affairs. The strife at first heated, soon became bitter, and even violent. The church seemed almost wholly to have forgotten her covenant with God and with each other; and God would appear well-nigh to have forsaken the church.

It is unnecessary to say that the cause of religion languished here; the heart of this people "waxed gross;" their ears grew "dull of hearing;" and the Lord's chosen became "an astonishment and a hissing" in the community,—until, at length, the state of things became so intolerable that the church, failing to secure the concurrence of the pastor in the calling of a Mutual Council, was obliged to resort to the extraordinary

* For a complete table of the annual accessions and removals, from the year 1816 to the present time (1867) see Appendix, Note III.

measure of an Ex-parte Council, by whose advice Mr. Chase was dismissed October 28, 1843, after a dreary pastorate of twenty-one and a half tempestuous months.

Although since those unpropitious years, God, in great mercy, has revisited his people, and sent upon them repeatedly the refreshing showers of his grace, yet, of the deplorable evils entailed upon the church by the hot haste and rash measures of that stormy period, some unwelcome traces are visible to this day, after the lapse of a quarter of a century.

But while we remember with unfeigned grief, the sore misfortunes which then befell the church, it affords us great gratification, and is an occasion of devout thankfulness to God, that previous to that time, through the long succession of one hundred and twenty-five years, the church had enjoyed almost an unbroken peace. To an unusual degree, this church and community had borne the character of a united, happy, and prosperous people. Dr. Phelps, alluding to the time when he entered upon his ministry here, says:—"The church and parish had long been distinguished for the peace, quiet, and harmony which had existed among themselves. It was often said to me, by ministers and others, that they regarded West Brookfield as the best congregation in the country. They were proverbially a ministerial people; and I found them so during the whole of my residence among them." Let us hope that such is to be our record in the years and generations to come.

For a short time after Mr. Chase's dismission, he ministered to a portion of the church and congregation who worshiped in what was called Mr. Lamson's Hall. But, in less than a year, we find the church again united in harmonious action with reference to the settlement of another minister.

As regards the personal history of Mr. Chase, I have utterly failed to obtain any satisfactory information. Whence he came, where he was educated, whither he went, and whether or not he now survives, has not been definitely ascertained. He is believed, however, still to be living with his family at Plattsburgh, New York.

The ninth pastor was Rev. Leonard S. Parker. He was born December 6, 1812, at Dunbarton, New Hampshire; fitted for college at the Boston Latin School, and entered Dartmouth College in 1832; but, on account of ill health, left before the time of graduation. In both of these institutions, as a scholar he ranked first in his class. He studied four years at Oberlin Collegiate Institute; was approbated to preach by the Lorain County Association, Ohio, in 1837, and was ordained as an Evangelist at Fitchville, Ohio, December 16, of the same year. He was installed first pastor of the Congregational Church in Mansfield, Ohio, September 9, 1838, where he continued a little more than two years. December 28, 1840, he was installed pastor of High Street Church, Providence, Rhode Island and was dismissed by reason of failure of health, October 9, 1843. He was installed pastor of this church December 19, 1844. The public exercises were as follows:—

Invocation and reading of the Scriptures by Rev. (now Dr.) Nahum Gale of the East Congregational Church, Ware; sermon by Rev. Thomas Snell, D. D. of North Brookfield; installing prayer by Rev. John Fiske, D. D. of New Braintree; charge to the pastor by Rev. D. R. Austin of Sturbridge; right hand of fellowship by Rev. Lyman Whiting of Brookfield (South Parish); address to the people by Rev. Levi Packard of Spencer; and concluding prayer by Rev. James Kimball of Oakham.

Mr. Parker's ministry here was begun under the most trying and discouraging circumstances. He found both the church and the society rent in twain on the subject of slavery, and the whole community in a pitiable state of agitation. Among his first acts as pastor was the introduction of a series of resolutions upon slavery, condemning in the strongest terms that system of oppression as "a flagrant sin in the sight of God, and an enormous injury to man." These resolutions were adopted by the church, January 16, 1845.

But the fires of passion could not in a moment be stayed. It was a time of "strong delusion" in this whole region of country. Under the cloak of zeal against the system of slavery, a fierce attack was made in many quarters upon the sacred institutions of religion. Conventions professedly called in the interests of *anti-slavery*, partook largely of the character of *anti-Christian* conventions. The Bible was subjected to an unfair criticism; the sanctity of the Sabbath called in question; the Church grossly slandered, and the Ministry maligned.

It was in this, as in too many churches of the Commonwealth, a time of great spiritual dearth. From July 7, 1839, to November 1, 1846, a period of more than seven years, including the last two years of the ministry of Mr. Horton, the whole of the ministry of Mr. Chase, and nearly the first two years of the ministry of Mr. Parker, there was *not one addition* to the church by profession. No other such period can be shown in our entire history; no time half so dark, distressing and mournful for the cause of Christ and the prosperity of Zion. But, thanks to Sovereign Grace under the gentle and discreet administration of Mr. Parker rancor of feeling was greatly subdued, and happier days began to break upon this sadly divided and sorely afflicted people.

In the latter part of 1846, four persons made a profession of their faith, and joined the church. In 1848 there came a refreshing which must have been truly delightful after the barrenness of the preceding years, and nineteen were gathered into the church as the fruit. The total accession to the church, during Mr. Parker's pastorate, was SIXTY-EIGHT, of whom twenty-seven were admitted on profession. He was dismissed April 7, 1851, having held the pastoral office a little more than six years.

He was installed pastor of the Winter Street church, Haverhill, June 1, 1853; and was dismissed March 26, 1860. The following year, February 20, he was installed over the First Church in Derry, New Hampshire, where he yet remains.

The publications of Mr. Parker, aside from stated correspondence for the weekly religious press, are; "Thoughts on Temperance," Providence, 1841; "A Farewell Sermon," Providence, 1843; "A Plea for Missions," West Brookfield, 1846; "A Good Name"—two Discourses addressed to the Young Men of West Brookfield, 1848; and "A Sermon on the day of the Annual State Fast," Derry, 1865.

The church remained without a pastor for about a year and a half, when the tenth pastor, Rev. Swift Byington, succeeded to the office. He was ordained and installed here November 17, 1852. The council was composed of messengers from the churches in New Braintree, North Brookfield, Brookfield, Warren, Ware Village, Spencer, Oakham, Old South Church, Reading, and Pine Street Church, Boston; also Rev. Messrs. Gilbert and Grannis of West Brookfield.

The ordination services were as follows:—Invocation and reading of the Scriptures by Rev. T. G. Colton of Ware Village; prayer by Rev. John Fiske, D. D. of New Braintree; sermon by Rev. (now Dr.) Henry M. Dexter of Boston; ordaining prayer by Rev. Levi Packard of Spencer; charge to the pastor by Rev. Lyman Whiting of Reading; right hand of fellowship by Rev. C. Cushing, colleague pastor North Brookfield; address to the people by Rev. Thomas Snell, D. D. of North Brookfield; and concluding prayer by Rev. James Kimball of Oakham.

Mr. Byington was born in Bristol, Connecticut, February 4, 1824; studied at East Hartford, Connecticut, Philadelphia and Providence, Pennsylvania, as a boy; fitted for college with Rev. Merrill Richardson, now of Worcester; and was graduated at Yale College in 1847. His Theological studies were pursued at New Haven and Andover; and he received his license to preach at East Haddam, Connecticut, in 1849. Although his whole ministry here was, he says, "an effort not to reap, but to sow deeply good seed," yet it pleased the Lord of the harvest to permit him to see at least some of the fruits of his own faithful labors. At two different seasons, particularly, there were cheering indications of the Spirit's presence and power, when God crowned his efforts with success, and gave him souls for his hire. In 1854 *fifteen*, and in 1858,—the last year of his ministry,—*seventeen*, were added to the church on profession of faith; and, during the six years in which he ministered to this people, the church received an aggregate of SEVENTY members, forty-six of whom united by profession. At his own request, the pastoral relation was dissolved November 1, 1858. After leaving this place, he preached in North ambridge six months, three years in North Woburn, and served one year as acting colleague pastor with Dr. Blagden, of the Old South Church, Boston. In 1864, July 6, he was installed pastor of the Congregational Church in Stoneham, where he still continues to labor.

Within eight months from the dismission of Mr. Byington, the eleventh pastor, Rev. Christopher M. Cordley, was settled. He was born in Oxford, England, January 2, 1821; removed at an early age to Nottingham, and, when about twelve years old, emigrated with his parents to this country, while employed as clerk of a store in Ann Arbor, Michigan, he prepared himself, with little help from others, for Western Reserve College, Hudson, Ohio, at which institution he was graduated in 1844 with the highest honors of his class. Having devoted the next three years to the study of theology at New Haven and Andover, he spent the winter of 1847 and 1848 in preaching at Montreal, Canada. In August 1849 he was ordained in Hopkinton, New Hampshire, and was called from the pastorate of that church to West Randolph, Massachusetts, where he was installed in March, 1852, and whence he was dismissed in November, 1858. He was installed pastor of this church June 28, 1859.

The services of the installation were as follows: Invocation and reading of the Scriptures by Rev. William. H. Beecher of North Brookfield, (Union Church); prayer by Rev. A. E. P. Perkins of Ware; sermon by Rev. R. S. Storrs, D. D. of Braintree; installing prayer by Rev. Martin Tupper of Hardwick; charge to the pastor by Rev. Joseph Vaill, D. D. of Palmer; right hand of fellowship by Rev. C. Cushing of North Brookfield; address to the people by Rev. Swift Byington, former pastor; concluding prayer by Rev. S. S. Smith of Warren.

The ministry of Mr. Cordley here was brief, and not altogether happy. He retired from the pastoral office, June 23, 1862, three years, wanting five days, from the day of his installation, during which time there were THIRTY-EIGHT accessions to the church, of whom eight only were admitted upon profession. But, during his short pastorate, Mr. Cordley rendered the church an exceedingly important service. By untiring patience and untold labor, such as none but a man of his energy would ever have consented to endure, and with characteristic accuracy and ingenuity, he prepared and published a complete catalogue of the members of this church, with an alphabetical index, from the year 1758 to 1861, embracing the entire period concerning which we have anything that can be called records.

By the aid of this catalogue, we can easily find out the full name of almost every person who has united with this church, whether by profession or by letter, during the last hundred years; when and whence each was received, and when and how dismissed, together with dates of marriages and deaths. Considering the meagreness of our early records, the work thus accomplished is a marvel. It is something which not one man in ten thousand would ever have undertaken, or, if they had undertaken, would ever have completed. It will long stand a witness of his persevering industry. It has proved of essential service in the preparation of the present discourse; and it is not too much to say that by the production of that catalogue Mr. Cordley conferred upon the church a lasting benefit, for which his name deserves to be had in perpetual remembrance by successive generations.

From this place he went to Lawrence, Massachusetts, and was installed pastor of the Central Church in that city in October, 1862; where, after a protracted and painful illness, he died June 26, 1866, aged forty-five years. Mr. Cordley was a man of exceeding independence of mind, of inflexible firmness, and of great daring. By his brethren in the ministry he was highly esteemed as an able and faithful minister, an accomplished scholar, an earnest Christian, and a man of rare personal worth.

From a manuscript biographical sketch and obituary, prepared by Professor Park of Andover, soon after Mr. Cordley's decease, and to which I am indebted for most of the facts already presented in relation to his personal history, I take the following extract having reference to the last sickness of our departed brother:—"In the progress of his disease, his trust in his Redeemer remained unfaltering, and he moved forward like a brave soldier with the assurance that the last enemy that shall be destroyed is death. His mind was often wandering, but the name of Jesus would call it back to its old paths. In his delirium he would be sometimes agitated, but the voice of prayer would soothe him into rest; and when the halls of his reason seemed to be left vacant, one of the sweet songs of Zion would call his reason back to its deserted home."

The present pastor was graduated at Yale College in 1860; studied theology two years at Union Seminary, New York, and a third year at Andover, where he was graduated in 1863. On the 12th, of April of that year,—four months previous to graduation,—he commenced to preach in this pulpit, and from that time, for nearly a year and a half, continued to act as stated supply till the day of his ordination as pastor October 4, 1864, a call having been extended the previous March. The council was organized by the choice of Rev. C. Cushing, moderator, and Rev. J. Coit, scribe. The public services of ordination were as follows:—Invocation by Rev. John H. Gurney of New Braintree; reading of the Scriptures by Rev. E. L. Jaggar of Warren; prayer by Rev. F. N. Peloubet of Oakham; sermon by Rev. E. C. Jones of Southington, Connecticut; ordaining prayer by Rev. L. S. Parker of Derry, New Hampshire; charge to the pastor by Rev. Luther Keene of North Brookfield; right hand of fellowship by Rev. Joshua Coit of Brookfield; address to the people by Rev. Swift Byington of Stoneham; and concluding prayer by Rev. Francis Horton of Barrington, Rhode Island.

These last years have been crowned with God's goodness in a peculiar manner, and have been freighted with most precious blessings to the church. As already intimated, for nearly thirty years previous to 1864, the membership of the church steadily diminished. Although within that time, there were, as we have seen, several happy seasons of spiritual quickening, yet those revivals were not of sufficient extent and power to repair the ordinary yearly waste from removals and deaths; so that on January 1, 1864, the church had become reduced to two hundred and twenty-nine members. By the decease and dismission of several, and by the erasure of some twenty-five names of persons who had been many years absent and unreported, this number was still further reduced to *one hundred and* *ninety-one*, which was the membership of the church when the present pastor was ordained.*

In the winter of 1863 and 1864 God kindly poured out His spirit in gentle and delightful showers, which continued to be distilled upon us through the succeeding spring, and into the summer, so that on the first Sabbath in November 1864, at the first communion after his ordination, and the first time he ever officiated at the Lord's table, the pastor had the undeserved privilege of welcoming *twenty-five* persons,—mostly young,—to the sacramental cup and loaf, and the happy fellowship of believers. As the fruit of that revival, or of the interest awakened and continued by it, eighteen more were subsequently received, making in all *forty-three.* But the revival of the present year is especially worthy of record. A short time previous to the Week of Prayer,—the first week in January—there were some signs of increasing fervor and expectancy on the part of the church. The Week of Prayer was observed by holding meetings in rotation in the several districts of the town, at each of which a number of brethren from the other districts, with the pastor, were present. By these meetings, and the accompanying personal efforts, the religious interest was quite sensibly increased, and the attention of a few impenitent persons arrested. This interest continued very gradually to deepen and extend with most happy results, until the middle of March, when the revival was greatly promoted by a Protracted Meeting commencing on Wednesday, March 13, and continuing three days, during which the pastor received efficient co-

* See Appendix, Note IV.

operation and aid from his brethren in the ministry from neighboring towns.

This meeting was followed, on the succeeding Saturday and Sunday, by the earnest and judicious labors of Rev. I. P. Langworthy of Chelsea; who also assisted the pastor on one subsequent Sabbath. By the signal blessing of God upon the direct, pungent preaching, upon the frequent prayer meetings, inquiry meetings, and extraordinary personal efforts, of that memorable week, many became anxious for the salvation of their souls, and not a few found peace at the cross. From that time onward, for many gracious weeks, the spirit of God moved upon this people with a mighty energy. Great fear came on many, and among them some who had long rebelled against God, and had even denied the truths of revelation. Religion was the almost universal topic of conversation; and this whole community felt the pulse of a quickened life.

As the rich fruit of this work of grace *sixty-three* persons, of an average age of thirty-four years, have already connected themselves with the church by profession. Of these *fifty-one* were received on the first Sabbath in July—a day long to be remembered,—thirty-five are heads of families, nine of whom are above sixty years of age, and one is more than seventy years.

The whole number received into the church during the three years of the present pastorate is ONE HUNDRED AND THIRTY-TWO, of whom one hundred and six were on profession of faith. The membership of the church, at this time, is *three hundred and two.* The oldest surviving member is ninety-four years old, the youngest, twelve.

Respecting the whole number who have belonged to the

church from its first existence, of those who were received during the first forty years of our history, only forty-seven names have been saved from oblivion. Since the year 1758, there have been admitted one thousand two hundred and ninety-eight different persons, making a total catalogue at the present time, of *one thousand three hundred and forty-five names.* Of this number, so near as can be determined, not more than six hundred and fifty are living to-day. More than half have already passed on into eternity.

THE DEACONS OF THE CHURCH.

Deacon Henry Gilbert stands at the head of the list. He is supposed to have been a descendant of Sir Humphrey Gilbert, who was an English navigator, and half-brother of Sir Walter Raleigh, born in Dartmouth in 1539, and sometimes called the "father of western colonization." He was, undoubtedly, the *first* man who received the office of deacon in this church. By special vote passed December 14, 1721, he was privileged to occupy, in the then new meeting-house, "a pue next to ye ministry pue." He was probably among the pioneer settlers of Brookfield, and was, evidently one of the foremost men of the place in his day; for we find him often associated with Hon. Jedediah Foster as a leader in the more important measures of Town and Church at that early period. He died August 17, 1740.

Deacon John Gilbert, son of Deacon Henry Gilbert, appears also to have held the office from the first year of the existence of the church. The second vote that appears upon the church records now extant, bearing date May 14, 1758, relates to him; when it was "Voted to send to assist in the ordination of Mr. Nathan Fiske. Mr. Jedediah Foster and Deacon Gilbert were chosen delegates." This is the first mention made of a deacon on our existing records. He continued in the office for half a century, resigning October 14, 1767, one hundred years ago almost to a day. He died June 12, 1779, aged ninety. He was undoubtedly the man who occupied what is called "Gilbert's Fort."

Joshua Dodge, though called deacon, probably never held that office in this church. The earliest vote of the church that has come down to us, is dated May 12, 1758, and is in the words following:—"Voted that Joshua Dodge, a member of ye church of England, shall have ye privilege of occasional communion." Thirteen years later, in 1771, by special permission, he was also allowed "to act with ye church in ye choice of a minister," he having "promised that he would be at proportionable charges with the people." He died April 23, 1793, at the age of ninety-two.

Deacon Joseph Jennings is mentioned as early as 1721. On December 14 of that year the town voted that he "have a pue next to Deacon Henry Gilbert's."

Deacon Comfort Barnes died January 17, 1748, aged forty-two years.

Deacon John Cutler. The date of his election to the office in *this* church cannot be determined, but his name appears, May 28, 1752, among the twenty-six male signers of the covenant at the organization of the Second Church of Christ in Brookfield, now the First Church in North Brookfield. In December 1753, he was chosen *first* deacon of that church.*

---

* Dr. Snell's "Historical and Centennial Discourses," p. 28, 29, and his Appendix, (C).

He is supposed shortly afterwards to have removed from the town; but when or where he died has not been ascertained.

Deacon Jedediah Foster, was born at Andover, Massachusetts; was graduated at Harvard University in 1744, and shortly after settled in Brookfield. He was elected deacon October 18, 1759. The record of this date reads:—"At a church meeting Jedediah Foster, Esq., was made choice of for a deacon. Suspended his answer till y[e] church consented to introduce Tate and Brady's Psalms upon trial; then gave it in the affirmative." Deacon Foster was not only the chief man of his time in matters of Church and Town, but also stood in the front rank of the men of the Commonwealth and Country. In 1751 he was appointed Major of forces raised for the defence of the country against the threatened invasion of the French. He was a member of the "Provincial Congress," and, when hostilities commenced with Great Britain, he was elevated to the office of Colonel. In 1755, he became a member of the Supreme Council, and afterward Judge of Probate and of the Supreme Court. In March, 1779, in the Convention at Cambridge, he was a member of the Committee chosen for the purpose of drafting a Constitution. Through his life, he enjoyed the confidence of the inhabitants of this Town and County, perhaps beyond any man who ever lived here, unless it be his own son, the Hon. Dwight Foster, who held successively and with honor the offices of High Sheriff of Worcester County, Chief Justice of the Court of Common Pleas, Member of Congress, and United States Senator. Yonder hill which bears his name is not more enduring than the fame and deeds of him who lived upon it. He resigned his office as deacon December 12, 1776, and died three years later, October 17, 1779, aged fifty-five. Dr. Nathan Fiske, pastor of the Third Church in Brookfield (South Parish), preached his funeral sermon, which was published. With great difficulty one can now decipher upon the time-worn stone that marks his resting-place in the Old Burying Ground, the inscription:—

> " The boast of Heraldry, the pomp of Power,
> " And all that Wisdom, all that Wealth e'er gave,
> " Await alike the inevitable hour;
> " The Paths of Glory lead but to the Grave."

Deacon Thaddeus Cutler united with this church November 1, 1761, and was elected deacon March 13, 1763. On September 20, 1767, he declined to continue longer in that office, when thanks for past services were voted him by the church. Scarcely more than three months after being relieved from his official duties, he was released from earth. He died January 2, 1768.

Deacon Othniel Gilbert became a member of this church September 7, 1766, and was chosen deacon October 14, 1767. In November 1788, " on account of Infirmity of Body," he retired from the office, having discharged its duties twenty-one years. He died February 6, 1795, in the sixty-eighth year of his age.

Deacon Thomas Rich was received into this church by letter from New Braintree in 1759, and was made deacon October 14, 1767. Six or eight years later he removed to Western (Warren), where he died February 16, 1803, aged seventy-four.

Deacon Joseph Cutler was " descended from Sir Gervase Cutler, of Norfolkshire, England, three of whose sons, according to tradition, came over to this country previous to 1640," and was father of the late Hon. Pliny Cutler, who, for many years, was a successful merchant in Boston, and a deacon of the Old South Church in that city, and who died in this town August 14, of the present year. He united with this church May 23, 1762. He was chosen deacon October 9, 1776, and "took ye matter under consideration." He signified his acceptance of the office not till December 12, of the same year, on the resignation of Judge Foster. "His views and habits were of the strict Puritan stamp. All work of man and beast upon his farm ceased on Saturday afternoon, an hour before sunset; the men shaved themselves and prepared for holy time before the sun went down; the work within doors was also completed, even to the preparing of the food for the following day; and from the going down of the sun on the eve of the Sabbath to the going down of the sun on the Sabbath day, no work, excepting that of absolute necessity and mercy, not even the making of a bed nor the sweeping of a room, was allowed. The whole time was devoted to rest, and to the solemn duties of religion. Although he lived three miles from the place of worship, yet he was ever promptly there, with all his family, morning and afternoon; neither heat, nor cold, nor storm, being able to turn his steadfast steps from the sanctuary of God."* At his own request, "on account of age, and infirmity of body," he was released from the duties of his office June 20, 1809, and died August 20, 1825, aged eighty-six. Upon his tombstone we read:—

"In God's own arms he left the breath,
Which God's own Spirit gave,
His was the noblest road to death,
And his the sweetest grave."

Deacon Levi Gilbert united with this church May 28, 1775; was chosen deacon December 11, 1788; and died in office

*Portraits of Eminent Americans, Vol. I. pp. 327, 328.

April 5, 1816, in the sixty-sixth year of his age. The slab that indicates the place of his burial tells us:—

> "Humble and meek a lowly path he trod,
> And while he liv'd on earth, he walk'd with God;
> Good without show, obliging without art,
> His speech the faithful language of his heart;
> His hope was grace, and his delight was prayer,
> His aim was Heaven; O! may we enter there."

Deacon Samuel Barnes became a member of this church November 29, 1789, and was elected deacon June 20, 1809. He resigned the office "on account of age and infirmity," November 10, 1819, and died January 27, 1833, at the age of seventy-five.

Deacon John Ross united with this church July 16, 1780. He was elected to the office of deacon June 20, 1809, and relinquished its duties November 27, 1828. He died October 16, 1846, aged eighty-seven.

Deacon Nathan Bucknam Ellis was a son of Asa Ellis, a deacon of the church in East Medway, and Margaret Bucknam, a daughter of Rev. Nathan Bucknam, who was pastor of the church in East Medway for more than seventy years. He removed to this place from East Medway and joined this church November 4, 1792. He was chosen deacon July 3, 1816; and died September 6, 1819, in the fifty-sixth year of his age. It was he who, in conjunction with others in this parish, set up a fulling-mill, and carried on a somewhat extensive business for those days, and especially excelled in the art of coloring cloth. Whitney* in his History, published in 1793, makes special mention of this Company. He says; "About five thousand yards of cloth are annually dressed at

* History of the County of Worcester, p. 79.

these works. These men have obtained the art of coloring scarlet, which competent judges pronounce equal to any which is imported; an art which few in this Commonwealth have attained unto."

Deacon John Wood united with this church December 7, 1817, and was chosen deacon November 10, 1819. He resigned the office March 14, 1832, and was dismissed April 7, 1833, and recommended to the First Presbyterian Church in Geneva, New York, at that time under the pastoral care of Rev. (now Dr.) Eliakim Phelps. In the Fall of 1835 he removed to Ann Arbor, Michigan, and thence, in June, 1837, to Iosco, Livingston County, of the same state, where he was one of the first settlers, (his son being the *first*) and the second land owner in the town. The *first religious meeting* ever held in Iosco was held in his house. In the Spring of 1845, he removed to the town of Putnam in the same County, and, in September following, united with the church in Pinckney, of which he was chosen deacon in August 1848, and continued in that office until a short time before his death. He died suddenly of heart disease March 23, 1864. His remains sleep by the side of those of his wife in Pinckney Church-yard.

Deacon Josiah Cary, son of Josiah and Mary (Moulton) Cary, was received into this church August 3, 1806, and was chosen to the office of deacon November 10, 1819. He resigned March 14, 1832, and in 1835, March 4, his relation was transferred to the Presbyterian Church, Princeton, New Jersey. In 1838, he removed to New York City, and was a member of the family of his son, Rev. J. Addison Cary, until the death of the latter in 1852, when he removed to Missouri, and lived with his daughter, wife of Rev. A. V. Schenck, until his death March 8, 1861. He died at Saint

Charles, Missouri, "in the full assurance of a blessed immortality," aged seventy-seven.

Deacon Alfred White, son of Asa and Anna White, and a lineal descendant in the fifth generation from Peregrine White, was born in this town July 25, 1785; united with this church May 23, 1813; and was chosen deacon November 10, 1819. Although, for a number of years past, relieved from the active duties of the office, he still occasionally officiates at the Lord's table. He is one of the oldest surviving members of the church, as also among the oldest citizens of the town. But, notwithstanding his advanced age, he is an habitual attendant upon the public worship of God's house on the Sabbath, and is here with us to-day, not an unmoved spectator of these commemorative services. An occasion of solemn and tender interest, and of grateful recollections, on the 15th of February last, was the celebration, in the vestry of this church, of the sixtieth anniversary of his marriage.

Deacon William Spooner was one of the fifty-one persons who united by profession with this church December 13, 1818. He was elected deacon November 27, 1828. He was dismissed April 7, 1833, to the church in Oakham, whence he was received again July 30, 1837. In 1851 he removed to Springfield, Massachusetts, where he died February 13, 1865, in his sixty-eighth year. His remains were brought to this town, and deposited in the cemetery here, the funeral services being conducted in this church. At his grave we read the simple, fitting inscription, "*There is sweet rest in Heaven.*"

Deacon Reuben Blair, Jr., was also among the fifty-one who, here in these aisles, united with the church on the same Sabbath, December 13, 1818. He was chosen deacon January 27, 1833, and died August 2, 1859, aged seventy-four.

Deacon Jairus Abbott, was received into this church from the church in Western (Warren), January 21, 1827, and was chosen deacon January 27, 1833. In May 12, 1834, he was dismissed to the Evangelical Congregational Church in the South Parish (now Brookfield), where he died March 18, 1850, at the age of threescore and ten years.

Deacon Josiah Henshaw, son of Josiah and Sarah (Phipps) Henshaw, united with this church September 29, 1816, and was elected to the office of deacon January 27, 1833. Of an ardent temperament, and of radical views and feelings, a warm friend of the enslaved negro, an earnest advocate of freedom, and impatient of delay, in the anti-slavery excitement of 1840 and onwards, he was easily led into some errors of opinion and indiscretions of conduct, which brought him into unhappy collision with the majority of the church, resulting, finally, in his excommunication, January 26, 1843.

Deacon Baxter Ellis, son of Deacon Nathan B. and Thankful (Barritt) Ellis, united with this church in August 1818, and was chosen deacon June 16, 1845. He retired from the active duties of the office June 5, 1851, and died October 8, 1866, in the seventy-fifth year of his age.

Deacon Jacob Dupee, son of Elias and Abigail Dupee, was born in Charlestown, Massachusetts, November 11, 1800. He removed to this town in 1827; was hopefully converted in the revival of 1835, and united with this church May 3, of the same year. He was chosen deacon June 16, 1845~~, and is still discharging the duties of the office~~.

Deacon Liberty Sampson, son of Daniel and Achsah (Snow) Sampson, united with this church by profession January 6, 1839, and was elected to the office June 16, 1845. He died October 15, 1858, aged thirty-eight.

Deacon Solomon L. Barnes, son of Ezra and Lucy (Caruth) Barnes, united with this church by letter from Ware (West), May 7, 1837. In November 1854 he was chosen deacon, the duties of which office he is still performing.

Deacon Moses Hall, son of Moses and Elizabeth Hall, was born in Spencer, Massachusetts, November 4, 1816, and removed to this town in 1840. In July 1853, he united with this church, and was chosen deacon in November of the following year. On removing from the place, he resigned the office, and his resignation was accepted April 9, 1863. He was recommended to the Congregational Church in Wethersfield, Connecticut, May 31, 1864, whence he was received again May 5, 1865.*

Deacon Samuel Newell White, son of Deacon Alfred and Sarah (Gilbert) White, united with this church May 3, 1835, and was chosen deacon July 1, 1859. He resigned the office February 1, 1867.

Deacon Enos Gilbert son of Bethuel and Chloe (Hill) Gilbert, united with this church March 3, 1839, and was elected deacon April 21, 1865, the church, on the same day, having previously voted to limit the term of service to five years.† He still retains the office.

HOUSES OF WORSHIP.

The *first* meeting-house in Brookfield was situated on Foster's Hill, about half a mile south-east of the house in which we are now assembled. It stood on the north side of the old road to Brookfield (South Parish), about equally distant from the house of the late Mr. Baxter Barnes, and the one now owned by Mr. D. H. Richardson.

---

* He was re-elected deacon November 1, 1867.

† This vote was rescinded November 1, 1867.

What were the dimensions of that rude, primitive structure we have no means of determining. It must have been built very soon after the first settlement of the town; for it was as early as 1675, on that dread night of August 4th—only fifteen years after the original grant was obtained from the General Court,—that the meeting-house, sharing the common fate of the town, was laid in ashes by the Indians.

Forty years passed away before another house of worship was erected. The place in which the people met during the thirty years that elapsed after their return from dispersion by the savages, and before the building of the second meeting-house, cannot now be ascertained. From their constant exposure to the attack of Indians, it is conjectured that, according to the customs of isolated settlements at that time, they met in some fortified place. As Gilbert's Fort was in the centre of the settlement, it seems probable that, for many years, the inhabitants gathered there for public worship.

For a few years previous to the building of the second meeting-house, however, it is altogether likely that they met in a house which stood nearly opposite to the residence of the late Mr. Baxter Barnes on Foster's Hill. A building called the town-house stood in that place; and, after the completion of the second meeting-house, it was given to Rev. Mr. Cheney, on the condition that he would release the town from that part of their contract in which they had agreed to build him a house.

The *second* meeting-house stood on the same site as the first.

On the 22d of November 1715, "The inhabitants of Brookfield agreed with the consent of ye Committee to build a meeting-house wherein to carry on ye worship of God; in form and manner as followeth: viz. 45 foott in Length, and 35 foott in wedht; and to put in Galery pieces so y[t] they may build Galeries when they shall have ocation; and to carry on the building of s[d] house as far as they can conveniently with y[r] Labour, and what shall be Required in money for y[e] carrying of s[d] work to be Raised by a Town Rate, and if any person or persons Refuse to Labour, Having suitable warning by y[e] Committee Hereafter mentioned, shall pay their proportion in Money. The Inhabitants Likewise agree to gett y[e] Timber this Winter." At the same meeting the Committee reported that they "unanimously agree that the inhabitants build a meeting-house wherein to attend the worship of God, which shall be sett up and erected in said place where formerly the meeting-house was built, near old John Ayres' house-lott lying near about the centre of the town."

January 4, 1717, a tax of thirty pounds was voted for glass and nails for the meeting-house, and eight pounds for window cases, and other public uses. Yet, four years later, the house seems not to have been quite completed, for under date April 18, 1721, we find the following unique vote, showing at least a rather doubtful solicitude for the physical comfort of the good deacons' wives of those days: "Granted a pue to be built on the left hand of the pulpit to be for the Deacons' wives, *s[d] wives to set in the pue during their natral life.*"

Also, on December 14, of the same year,

"*Voted,* That the select men lay out the land about the meeting-house, as it is Granted upon Record.

"*Voted,* To build up the seats in the body of y[e] meeting-house with good strong plain seats.

"*Voted,* To build a ministry pue on y[e] Right hand of y[e] pulpit, to the stairs of y[e] pulpit, to y[e] middle stud in y[e] window.

"*Voted,* That Henry Gilbert have a pue next to y[e] ministry pue.

"*Voted,* That Deacon Joseph Jennings have a pue next to Deacon Henry Gilbert's.

"*Voted,* That he that hath a pue granted in the meeting-house do pay to the town Treasurer forty shillings for each pue by the first day of April next coming, or else to forfeit their pues; and the money so paid in to be laid out to finish the meeting-house."

A careful regard was had, in those times, for age, and social rank and worth, as is shown by the following action of the town dated January 13, 1727:

"*Voted,* That the Committee y[t] shall be chosen to seat y[e] meeting-house shall have regard to age *(where it is honourable)*, and to estate, taking y[e] list y[t] Mr. Cheney's last Rate was made by for a rule, having also regard to men's *servicefulness* in the town.

"*Voted,* That it shall be left to five men to seat the meeting-house.

"*Voted,* That Elisha Rice, Samuel Barnes, Joseph Brabrook, Thomas Gilbert and Samuel Wheeler be of s[d] Committee to seat y[e] meeting-House.

"*Voted,* That the fore seat in y[e] front Gallery shall be equal with y[e] third seat in y[e] Body, and y[e] fore seat in y[e] side Gallery shall be equal with y[e] fourth seat in y[e] Body of y[e] meeting-house."

Thus a man's wealth and standing in society were pretty accurately indicated by the relative position of the seat which he occupied in the house of God, where "*the rich and poor meet together.*"

About forty years after the second meeting-house was built, it would appear to have suffered violence at the hands of some evil-minded and lawless men. For in a meeting of the town held September 30, 1754, "The question was asked by the moderator whether the town will effectually impour a committee to prosecute those persons who have *demolished the meeting-house* in the first parish, called the old meeting-house, in any Court, General or Executive, to final judgment and execution," or take any other measures for the settlement of the affair; which received a negative vote.

The *third* meeting-house was built in 1755, and stood near the spot where we are met to-day. January 22, 1755, the first Precint

Voted to "proceed to Build a meeting-house for Publick Worship at the turning of the County Rode near the north-east corner of a Plow-field belonging to John Barnes, being on the Plain in said first Precinct.

"*Voted*, That said meeting-house be built with timber and wood.

"*Voted*, That the meeting-house shall be forty-five feet in length, and thirty-five feet in width."

July 15, 1756,

"*Voted*, To sell the pew flour in the meeting-house to the Inhabitants of s[d] Precinct, preference to be made to those Persons who pay the largest tax, *provided they will give as much as others.*

"*Voted*, That seventeen Pews shall be made upon the flour of said meeting-house, and No More, adjoyning to the wall of said house.

"*Voted*, That Abner Gilbert be appointed to take Care of the Doors and Sweep the meeting-house, and if He except, he shall Sweep said house twelve times a year from this time, and oftener if need be, and that he shall receive as a reward twelve shilling at the end of the year."

This is the first intimation of the existence of a sexton. June 28, 1756—

"*Voted*, To build a Pulpit, Deacon's seat, and Ministerial Pew; also to build a body of seats having a Convenient Alley between them, and room on the back Side for a tear of Pews between the body of seats and the Alley before the Pews in the frunt Part of the meeting-house."

In September 3, 1759, it was

"*Voted*, To sell the front Gallery in the meeting-house to make into Pews.

"*Voted*, To Build the Gallery stairs, Lay the Gallery floors, Build the Brestwork, and three seats in the front, and two seats in each of the Side Galereys."

March 24, 1770, Captain Thomas Gilbert was appointed to provide a "Cushing for the pulpit, such as he shall think proper, and Charge the Precinct therewith." The luxury of a cushion having been introduced into the pulpit, the next thing was to put upon the rough interior of their sanctuary a higher touch of art. It was voted, November 14, 1761, "That the meeting-house shall be Lathed, Plaistered and whitewashed at the charge of said Precinct next year." Forty pounds were ordered to be raised for that purpose. As yet no liquid chime of Sabbath bell had broken here the stillness of the day of holy rest, or ever spoken its winning "welcome to the house of prayer."

That sweet and soul-awakening sound was reserved for a later generation. In a warrant for a meeting, to be held November 9, 1789, of "all the freeholders and other Inhabitants qualified by law to vote in Town meetings, living within the limits of the First Parish," there was an article,—"To see if the Parish will grant any money for the purpose of purchasing a Bell for the use of the Parish." But, at the meeting, the matter seems to have been passed over in silence; no action was taken upon it.

The next year (November 1, 1790) the Parish voted to choose a committee of five men to draw a plan for *enlarging* the meeting-house. This committee subsequently reported "that eight feet be built at each end of the meeting-house, and built into pews, &c.;" but the report was negatived. The opinion, doubtless, prevailed that the better policy would be to build anew. For, two years afterwards, it was decided to repair the old house by simply "patching the Ruff;" and at the same time (October 29, 1792,) they voted "to build a meeting-house for Publick worship on the land given to the first precinct in Brookfield by the late Lieutenant John Barnes for that purpose."

On the 17th of December following, it was agreed "to except one of the Plans for a meeting-house presented by the committee chosen for that purpose," and—

" *Voted*, That the meeting-house be built by the sale of the pews, if the same shall be sufficient, if not, the remaining sum to be assessed on the Polls and Estates of the Precinct."

A committee of seven was chosen to superintend the sale of the pews, (as delineated in the plan adopted) and the building of the house; which committee subsequently (January 29, 1793) reported that they had sold the pews for eleven hundred and seven pounds. Arrangements were further made for procuring timber and other materials, and March 10, 1794, it was "voted to set the new meeting-house partly where the old one now stands."

Two months later the parish voted "that the new meeting-house stand on flat stones on the soil, as the ground is now staked out, and that the committee ask and provide for as many hands as shall be needed for raising the new meeting-house." Accordingly, the house in which we hold these services to-day soon began to rise; was finished the following year, and dedicated November 10, 1795, the sermon on the occasion being preached by Rev. Enos Hitchcock, D. D. of Providence, Rhode Island. The original dimensions of the house, as would appear from the plan which it was voted to adopt, were, length sixty-three feet, breadth fifty feet.

The old meeting-house was removed, so as to give place to the new, to "the south corner of the lot of land formerly owned by Nathaniel Gilbert, late of Brookfield, deceased," and was devoted to town and parish uses. In 1809 it was sold at "*publick vendue*" for the sum of one hundred and eighty-six pounds.

In the Spring of 1798 a second attempt was made to procure a bell, but, like the first, resulted in failure. But a better success was achieved the following year, when the parish raised the sum of four hundred dollars—half by subscription and half by tax—for the purchase of a Bell and an Eight Day Clock for the new meeting-house; the surplus money, should any remain, to be "appropriated to procure furniture for the Desk and Desk Window in said meeting-house." A bell of six hundred and seventy-one pounds weight was duly purchased of Mr. Paul Revere at Boston, and was "raised and hung," the whole at an expense of three hundred and forty-four dollars and fifty-six cents. For lack of funds the project of obtaining a clock was abandoned. (A clock, at that period, was an expensive piece of furniture.) It may be a matter of interest to know that the cost of transporting the bell from Boston to Brookfield, a distance of seventy miles, in those days of slow locomotion, was four dollars and fifty cents — pretty lean wages, one would think in these times of inflated currency, as the work must have consumed at least two or three days of time for man and team. The present bell was purchased in 1855. The first introduction of *stoves* here, as elsewhere, evidently did not meet with universal favor. The parish voted, December 8, 1818, "to raise the sum of one hundred and fifty dollars for the purpose of erecting two stoves in the meeting-house." But they immediately reconsidered this action, and voted "that individuals belonging to the parish be *permitted*, if they choose, to place a stove or stoves in the meeting-house." How soon thereafter this *desideratum* was obtained, does not appear.

In 1826 measures were taken to procure an *organ*, which in

due time, was accomplished. This instrument was replaced, in 1856, by a new and better one, which is still in use.

In 1838, forty-three years from the time of its erection, this house was thoroughly remodeled, at an outlay, apart from stoves, chandelier, and other incidentals, of five thousand four hundred and sixty-one dollars and sixty-eight cents. It was turned around to a right angle with its former position, and moved back about a rod in the rear of its original site. An addition was also built on each side of the old porch, the extent of the building, making the body of the house eighty feet in length, with a capacity, including gallery, for eight hundred sittings. Instead of the former cupola, a steeple ninety-two feet in height was erected, bearing the same vane that crowned the old meeting-house. Besides, a projection of six feet, with four pillars, was added in front; a new basement story was made, sixty-five by fifty-two feet, which, in 1840, was finished at a cost, inclusive of furniture for the vestry, of four hundred dollars, and divided into two apartments—one for a Vestry, and the other for a Town-house, which continued to be so used until our new and spacious Town Hall was completed in the spring of 1860. This house, as thus remodeled, was dedicated January 1, 1839. The introductory prayer on the occasion was offered by Rev. Mr. Smalley, of Worcester; reading of select portions of Scripture by Rev. Micah Stone of South Brookfield; sermon by Rev. Hubbard Winslow of Boston; prayer of dedication by Rev. John Fiske of New Braintree; concluding prayer by Rev. Dr. Snell of North Brookfield.

This house was again thoroughly retouched in 1849, and yet other alterations made a few years later, in the early part of the ministry of Mr. Byington, through the enterprise and energy of the ladies, as evinced by the following: At a meeting of the directors of the "Union Society" of West Brookfield in the Spring of 1854, it was

"*Voted,* That the said Society present, gratuitously, to the parish all the improvements they have made in the interior of the meeting-house, and embracing the pulpit, fourteen globe lamps, and clock."

In response to which the parish

"*Resolved,* That they accept the same; and that, in consideration of the courtesy and generosity of the Union Society in thus presenting those valuable and ornamental fixtures, the thanks of the parish be tendered to said Society, and that this resolve be entered on the records of the parish."

During the present year also, a few hundreds of dollars have been expended upon the exterior for painting and other needed repairs. The work of thoroughly renovating and beautifying the now marred and dingy *interior* has been reserved till after the one hundred and fiftieth anniversary only because the anniversary came *one year too soon.* It is confidently expected that the year 1868 will find us within a sanctuary rendered far more elegant and attractive by the introduction of some of the more modern improvements in church architecture.

MINISTERS FROM THE CHURCH AND PARISH.

Enos Hitchcock was born in 1744; was graduated at Harvard College in 1767; and was settled as colleague pastor with Rev. Mr. Chipman of Beverly, Massachusetts, in 1771, where he continued nine years.

In 1780 he became chaplain in the revolutionary army, which office he held till 1783. In that same year, (October 1st,) he was installed pastor of the Benevolent Congregational Church of Christ, in Providence, Rhode Island, which afterwards became a Unitarian church. In 1788 he received the degree of Doctor of Divinity. In 1802 his health failed, and on the 27th of February of the following year, consumption terminated his life, at the age of fifty-nine, in the twentieth year of his ministry at Providence.

Dr. Hitchcock prepared a catechism, called "The Parent's Assistant," and published several books upon education. Among his publications is "A Discourse delivered at the Ordination of the Rev. Jonathan Gould to the ministerial office in the Christian Church, at Standish, September 18, 1793." He also preached the sermon at the dedication of this house, November 10, 1795.

Joshua Crowell, son of Joshua and Mary (Field) Crowell, was born September 15, 1777. His parents were both members of this church until their death. He studied for a time at Leicester Academy, and also at Salem. He was converted under the labors of Rev. Elijah Bachelor, a Methodist minister who preached on circuit at the house of Widow Crowell, (Joshua's mother,) on "Ragged Hill;" soon became a Methodist itinerant preacher, and labored successfully for a number of years in several of the New England States, until 1809, soon after which he removed to Ware, where he resided for many years, partly engaged in secular pursuits. The last few years of his life were spent with his daughter in Sturbridge, where he died July 21, 1858, in the eighty-first year of his age, and fifty-seventh of his ministry. He was one of the founders and trustees of the Wesleyan Academy, Wilbraham.

Asa Kent was born May 9, 1780. Early consecrated to God by a devotedly pious mother, in the hope that he would become a preacher of the gospel, at the age of eighteen he yielded his heart to Christ; at twenty-one was licensed to exhort, and was immediately employed on the circuit in Vermont. The following year he was placed on another circuit in the same State, and revivals in various places attended his labors. Afterwards he was stationed at various points in Vermont; still later in Lynn, Massachusetts, and Bristol, Rhode Island.

In 1814 he was made Presiding Elder over the New London District, which office he held four years. Subsequently he preached at several important centers, as Providence, New Bedford, Newport, Charlestown, until 1838, when increasing infirmities compelled him to abandon the labors of a ministerial charge. He removed to New Bedford, where he lived, beloved and revered, the remainder of his days.

In 1840 he was chaplain to the house of correction in New Bedford, and after that, for four years, preached regularly once a Sabbath in some of the churches, and gave instruction in a Sabbath school. During his life he often enriched the columns of the Methodist religious journals with the productions of his ready pen. His days were filled up with usefulness; and, calmly trusting in the atonement of Christ, he died at New Bedford, September 1, 1860, aged eighty.

Charles Gilbert, son of Nathaniel and Elizabeth Gilbert, was graduated at Dartmouth College in 1801, a classmate and intimate friend of Daniel Webster, with whom, after leaving college, he used to hold friendly correspondence. But death made him an early victim, and he died March 12, 1805, at the age of twenty-seven. His grave is in the Old Burying Ground. On his tombstone we read: "He had a collegiate education; had completed his theological studies, and commenced a preacher of the Gospel with pleasing prospects of success and usefulness; but they were soon blasted by death."

Caleb Sprague Henry, son of Silas Henry, was born at Rutland, Massachusetts, August 2, 1804, and removed with his father's family to West Brookfield in 1813. The main facts in his history are to be found in Appleton's New American Cyclopedia. He was graduated at Dartmouth College in 1825; studied theology at Andover and New Haven; was licensed to preach by the Brookfield Association in 1828, and was settled the following year as Congregational minister, at Greenfield, Massachusetts. From 1832 to 1835 he was associate pastor with the venerable Dr. Perkins, at West Hartford, Connecticut. In 1834 he published a pamphlet on the "Principles and Prospects of the Friends of Peace." About this time he also established a journal called the "American Advocate of Peace," which, after the first year, became the organ of the American Peace Society. In 1835 he was ordained in the Protestant Episcopal Church, by Bishop Onderdonk of New York; soon after which he became Professor of Intellectual and Moral Philosophy in Bristol College, Pennsylvania; which position he retained until 1837, when he removed to New York City, and, in conjunction with Dr. Hawks, established the New York Review. The same year the degree of Doctor of Divinity was conferred upon him by Geneva College, New York. He edited the Review until 1839, when he became Professor of Philosophy and History in the New York University. In 1847, in addition to the duties of his professorship, he took the rectorship of St. Clement's Church, New York. His health failing from overwork, he resigned the care of the church in 1851, retaining however his professorship, and performing, for some part of the time, the duties of the chancellorship of the University also. In 1852 ill health compelled him to resign his professorship, since which time, by the direction of physicians, he has lived in the country. His present place of residence is Newburgh on the Hudson.

Dr. Henry has published, besides the works already mentioned, a translation of Cousin's Lectures on Locke's "Essay on the Human Understanding," with notes and additional pieces, the work appearing under the title of "Cousin's Psychology," (1834,) and since revised and enlarged; also, a "Compendium of Christian Antiquities" (1837); "Moral and Philosophical Essays" (1839); an "Epitome of the History of Philosophy," translated from the French (1845); "Guizot's General History of Civilization, with Notes;" "Household Liturgy;" Taylor's "Manual of Ancient and Modern History," revised, with a chapter on the History of the United States (1845); "Dr. Oldham at Greystones and his Talk There" (1859); "Considerations upon the Elements and Conditions of Social Welfare and Human Progress" (1860); an Oration on "Patriotism and the Slaveholder's Rebellion" (1861); "Politics and the Pulpit," and many articles in the "Continental Monthly," and other journals, numerous addresses, etc.

Lucius Watson Clark, son of James and Jerusha (Marcy) Clark, was born in Mansfield, Connecticut, July 2, 1801; removed with his parents to this place in 1812; was converted under the ministry of Rev. Mr. Phelps in the revival of 1818, and united with this church December 13, of that year. He was graduated at Brown University in 1824; pursued his theological studies with Dr. Ide of Medway; was licensed to preach by the Mendon Association in 1826; was ordained pastor of the church in Wilbraham, (Massachusetts,) in 1829, where he continued three years. He was afterwards, for five years pastor at Plymouth, and five years at Amesbury; after which, on account of insufficient health, he labored only as temporary supply. Some eight or nine years previous to his death, he removed to Middlebury, Vermont, where he died of lung fever after only a few days' illness, January 2, 1854.

From an obituary published in the Boston Recorder soon after his death, I take the following brief passage:—"As a man, a friend, a Christian, they only knew his worth, who knew him well. Reliable, conscientious, and generous even to a fault; frank in his words, transparent in his motives, steadfast to principle, and to duty; kind, sympathizing, and true to his Master; a meek, humble and prayerful follower of the Lord Jesus Christ, whose earnest desire was that God be honored and men redeemed." Almost his last work on earth was to address a company of grieving mourners from the inspiring words, "Blessed are the dead which die in the Lord from henceforth: yea saith the spirit, that they may rest from their labors; and their works do follow them."

John C. Nichols, son of Isaac and Abigail (Cutler) Nichols, was born November 17, 1801. In the summer of 1818, he united with this church, and is still a member of it, having never removed his relation. He was graduated at Yale College in 1824; pursued his theological studies at New Haven; was licensed by the New Haven West Association in 1830, and, for three years following, was a Home Missionary in Canada. In the meantime,—in 1831,—he returned to the states, and was ordained in North Brookfield for his missionary work.

In 1834 he was installed pastor of the Second Church in

Stonington, Connecticut, and was dismissed in 1839. In 1840 he became pastor of the First Church in Lebanon, Connecticut, where, in 1855, he discontinued his labors on account of failing health. Soon afterwards he removed to Old Lyme, Connecticut, and there he has remained ever since, teaching and preaching, as health and opportunity have permitted.

Sewall Lamberton, son of Samuel D. and Lucy E. Lamberton, was born August 6, 1818. He was hopefully converted at the age of thirteen, and, the following year, was admitted to the communion of the Methodist Episcopal Church. During the years 1835 and 1836 he held license as an exhorter, and, in that capacity, labored more or less in different towns. April 24, 1837, he was licensed to preach at Chicopee Falls; after which his time was devoted to study and the work of the ministry, laboring at South Hadley, Palmer and Wilbraham, this State; and in Norwich, Enfield, East Windsor, Colchester, Haddam, and South Windsor, Connecticut, until bodily infirmity obliged him to relinquish, for the most part, ministerial duties.

In connection with his earlier labors, he spent two and a half or three years at the Wesleyan Academy, Wilbraham. In July, 1844, he became connected with the Providence Conference, and received his first ordination by vote of that body. Much of the time for twenty years past, he has been unable to perform regular ministerial service. Within that period he has spent several years in Southwick, preaching more or less for the different churches of that town. For the last five years he has lived in Westfield, where he still continues to preach occasionally.

Solomon B. Gilbert, son of Ezra and Ruth (Barnes) Gilbert, was born January 25, 1811; entered Amherst College in 1832, where having remained one year, he went to Bangor, Maine; studied for a time in the preparatory department, then entered the Theological Seminary in that place, where he was graduated in 1837. He was licensed to preach a short time previously by the Penobscot Association in Bangor. He was ordained as an Evangelist at Lyman, Maine, November 15, 1837. From thence he went to Newfield in the same State, where he was installed pastor in the spring of 1841. Three years later he accepted a call to Kennebunkport, Maine, where he preached without settlement till the spring of 1847, when he removed to Western New York and had charge of the church in Parma and Greece two years, and of the church in Fairport three years. In 1852 he returned to Massachusetts; subsequently spent a few months in Augusta, Maine, for the benefit of his health, acting meanwhile as city missionary, and in February, 1853, was installed pastor of the church in Prescott, Massachusetts, where he remained one year, when he accepted a call to Wendell, Massachusetts, and was installed in November, 1854. In December of the following year he went to Lyme, Ohio, where he preached until May 1857, when he was taken sick with congestion of the lungs, and died on the twenty-second of that month, after an illness of but one week. His remains repose in the cemetery at Lyme. Through life of a delicate constitution, his bodily sufferings during his last sickness were great, but his soul was at peace, and "he died praising the Lord."

William B. Bond, son of Thomas and Jemima (Bush) Bond, was born January 12, 1815; removed to Springfield at about the age of eleven years; fitted for college at Westfield Academy, and at a boarding-school in South Hadley, the principal of which was Rev. David R. Austin, afterward pastor of the church in Sturbridge. It was in this school that he experienced religion, in the summer of 1831. He was graduated at Amherst College in 1835; studied theology two years in Lane Seminary, Ohio, and graduated at New York in 1839; was licensed to preach by the Third Presbytery in New York, April 8, of the same year, and ordained pastor of the Congregational Church in Lee, Massachusetts, March 18, 1840, where he labored successfully during a ministry of about seven years, and was permitted to see a general revival of religion, as the result of which nearly one hundred persons united with the church by profession of their faith. He was installed pastor of the Second or North Congregational Church in St. Johnsbury, Vermont, October 15, 1847, where he remained about eleven years, during which time the church was blessed with two seasons of special religious interest, and about one hundred and twenty-five persons were added to its membership. On account of a failure of health, he was unable, for several years thereafter, to assume any charge. In February, 1865, he became acting pastor of the First Congregational Church, in Palmer, in the village of Thorndike, which still continues to be his field of labor.

Josiah Addison Cary, son of Deacon Josiah and Betsey (Henry) Cary, was born March 29, 1813. He united with this church September 2, 1827, when but fourteen years of age. He prepared for college at Hadley and Amherst academies, and was graduated a Amherst College in 1832, ranking among the foremost of his class for talent, scholarship, and piety. He had set his heart upon the missionary work, but the providence of God ordered otherwise. Soon after leaving college, he was appointed a professor in the New York Institution for the deaf and dumb. While thus engaged in that Institution, he, at the same time, carried on his theological studies, and was graduated at the Union Seminary in 1837. In 1839 he was licensed to preach by the Third Presbytery of New York; was ordained as an Evangelist at the Mercer Street Church in 1844; and installed in 1849 pastor of a Dutch Reformed Church, worshiping in Bleeker Chapel, New York, still continuing, however, to discharge his duties as instructor of the deaf and dumb. But these combined labors overtasked his strength, and after a little more than a year he was obliged to resign his pastorate in consequence of impaired health. In the spring of 1851 he visited the Island of Cuba, whence returning after an absence of two months with little benefit to his health, he was induced, by the hope that a change of residence might prove beneficial, to accept the appointment of superintendent of the Ohio Deaf and Dumb Asylum at Columbus. But this hope was a delusive one: for he had discharged the duties of his new and important trust less than one year, when he was thrown upon a sick bed from which he never rose. He died greatly lamented, at Columbus, August 7, 1852, having given nineteen years, or just one half of his life, to the instruction of the unfortunate deaf mute. Mr. Cary was a man of more than ordinary excellence of mind and character. In what estimation he was held by those who knew him is shown in various articles published, and resolutions passed, soon after his death. At a convention of the instructors of the deaf and dumb held at Columbus, among other resolutions that were adopted, were the following:—

"*Resolved,* That we deeply deplore the death of the Rev J. Addison Cary, the Superintendent of the Ohio Deaf and Dumb Asylum, both on account of his many amiable qualities which were so constantly manifested in all the relations of life, and that distinguished success which had attended his labors for the intellectual, moral and religious improvement of deaf mutes.

"*Resolved,* That we will ever treasure among the most sacred trusts of our memories the virtues of the departed, believing that his life presented a model as teacher and superintendent, rarely equalled, and never surpassed."

By the Board of Directors of the New York Institution in which Mr. Cary was for many years professor, it was

"*Resolved,* That in the lamented decease of Professor Cary, in the midst of his career of usefulness, the science of deaf mute instruction has been deprived of one of its most able and accomplished advocates, the cause of Christian benevolence of an earnest and devoted supporter, and the circle of his attached friends of one universally beloved for the many virtues of his personal character."

He died in the triumphs of faith, testifying, in the hour of his dissolution, to the sustaining power of the Christian religion. A son of Mr. Cary is now a member of Yale College.

William B. Stone, son of Francis and Hannah Stone, was born in North Brookfield, January 24, 1811. He removed with his parents to this parish when he was six years old. Through the influence of a Christian mother his mind was often seriously impressed, yet he experienced no deep and permanent change until, at the age of sixteen, under the preaching of Rev. Mr. Foot, his heart yielded to the claims of Christ, and he, together with twenty-four others, united with this church March 4, 1827. From the time that he consecrated his heart and life to God, he had a strong desire to preach the Gospel, but was not permitted to commence preparation for that work during his minority. At the age of twenty-two he began the study of Latin and Greek in preparation for college, teaching or laboring, meanwhile, a portion of each year, in order to procure pecuniary means for his education. He pursued his preparatory studies, for the most part, at Hadley Academy; and was graduated at Amherst College in 1839. He studied theology for a time at Andover, and completed his theological studies with Rev. George Trask of Warren. He was licensed to preach by the Brookfield Association in 1841; was ordained pastor of the Evangelical Congregational Church, Gardiner, Massachusetts, February 23, 1842, where he remained until August, 1850, when, partly by reason of ill health, and partly in consequence of the solicitation of his parents, he retired from the ministry, and took up his residence in this town, where he still lives, and is known as a thorough-going and prosperous farmer.

Austin Phelps, son of Rev. Dr. Eliakim and Mrs. Sarah (Adams) Phelps, was born in West Brookfield January 7, 1820. He was fitted for college by Rev. Dr. Dewey of Pittsfield, and Rev. Justus French of Geneva, New York; entered college at Geneva in 1833, when but thirteen years old, and was graduated with the highest honors at the University of Pennsylvania in 1837.

He was hopefully converted under the ministry of Rev. Albert Barnes, of Philadelphia, and joined the church of which he was pastor, in the summer of 1838. He studied theology partly in private, but mainly at the Seminaries in New York, New Haven, and Andover. He was licensed to preach by the Third Presbytery, of Philadelphia, in 1839, and on March 31, 1842 was ordained pastor of Pine Street Church, Boston, and closed his labors there in May, 1848, which was his only pastorate.

In September of the same year he was inaugurated Professor of Sacred Rhetoric at Andover, and has held that position ever since with marked ability and success; during which time more than five hundred pupils have enjoyed his instructions. He received the degree of Doctor of Divinity from Amherst College in 1846, when only twenty-six years of age.

He was married in September 1842 to Elizabeth, eldest daughter of Professor Moses Stuart of Andover. She died in November 1852. She was the authoress of "The Sunny Side," &c., and a writer of great promise. In April, 1855, he was married to her sister Mary Stuart, who died in September, 1856. His present wife, to whom he was married in June, 1858, is Mary, youngest daughter of Samuel Johnson, Esq., of Boston, and grand-daughter of Captain Howe, formerly well known as a citizen of South Brookfield.

Although yet in middle life, the productions of Professor Phelps' pen are already somewhat numerous, and by no means wanting in merit. He was joint editor, with Professor Park and Dr. Lowell Mason, of "The Sabbath Hymn Book," which is now used in the "Service of Song" by more than a thousand churches; joint author, with Professor Park and Rev. D. L. Furber, of "Hymns and Choirs," which is a History and General Discussion of Hymnology.

That valuable little book, "The Still Hour, or, Communion with God" is also from his pen. It was originally a sermon prepared for his people in Boston in the ordinary course of his ministry there. The great popularity of this work is shown by the fact that it has had a circulation of more than forty thousand in this country, and more than sixty thousand in England and France.

A more recent publication of his is "The New Birth."

Add to these, various articles in the Bibliotheca Sacra; an oration before the Porter Rhetorical Society of Andover; a sermon before the Pastoral Association of Massachusetts; a sermon before the Massachusetts Convention of Congregational Ministers, and the Election Sermon before the Legislature of Massachusetts in 1861.

Besides, Professor Phelps has frequently preached at Ordinations, Dedications, and on other public occasions. And yet, with characteristic humility, he writes: "A retrospect of one's life, from the 'silent shore' on which I seem to myself to have been walking, in my infirmity, these five years past, does on awaken self-gratulation." His religious history, he says, "contains nothing of value to others but the old story of a faithful Saviour." He adds: "My purpose to be a minister, I trace back distinctly to my earliest years in Brookfield. It was breathed into me by the example and prayers of my father and mother. As Gibbon says of Christianity, '*it was in the atmosphere*' of my early home. In fact, I suspect that I was born with it."

Nathaniel Spear, eldest son of Nathaniel and Sarah (Arnold) Spear, was born September 4, 1814. From the age of sixteen he served an apprenticeship of five years to the tailor's trade, at the expiration of which time he commenced a course of study, and at the age of twenty-four was prepared for college. But, on account of the failure of his health, he abandoned his purpose of gaining a liberal education. He removed into Western New York, where he was largely instrumental in establishing a new church. After a time he was called to labor in the employ of the Bible Society, and at length, under the auspices of the American Tract and Bible Societies in conjunction, he was engaged for six years in presenting the cause of these Societies among the churches of north-eastern Pennsylvania, since which time the Presbytery of Northumberland, Pennsylvania, (O. S.,) has ordained him pastor of *three* churches within the bounds of that Presbytery, and under the care of the Domestic Missionary Society. These churches are at Rohrsburg, Sugar Loaf and Orangeville, the latter being his place of residence.

Harrison Otis Howland, son of Southworth and Esther (Allen) Howland, was born January 25, 1813. He prepared for college at Leicester Academy; was graduated at Amherst College in 1841, and at the Union Theological Seminary, New York city in 1844. He was ordained in Ashland, New York, in 1846, and has since been pastor of churches in Warner and Chester, New Hampshire, and in Girard, Erie County, Pennsylvania, where he now resides, though not as settled pastor.

William Ware Howland, half-brother of the preceding, was born February 25, 1817. His mother was Mary Ware, daughter of Dr. Samuel Ware, who, for more than fifteen years, was pastor of the First Church in Ware. He was graduated at Amherst College in 1841, and at Union Seminary, New York, in 1845. In the autumn of the same year he was ordained at South Hadley, and sailed from Boston as a missionary to Ceylon under the auspices of the A. B. C. F. M. From that time to the present—a period of twenty-two years—he has been stationed at Batticotta. In the meantime he has once visited this country. Letters from him frequently appear in the columns of the "Missionary Herald." Two of his sons, William and Samuel, are now members of the Sophomore class in Amherst College.

Edwin Gilbert, son of Harvey and Phydema Gilbert, was

born February 11, 1824; studied at Chester, Farmington and Austinburgh, Ohio, and completed his studies with Horatio Foote at Quincy, Illinois, in the summer of 1850; and in the autumn following was ordained at Payson, Illinois. He had been recommended as a minister the previous year, and from that time until the fall of 1852 preached at Concord, Morgan County, Illinois. In 1857 and 1858 he preached at Hampden, Ohio; in 1859 at Geneva in the same State, where he died May 13, 1860, at the age of thirty-six. During the last fifteen years of his life he was a great sufferer from a complication of diseases, terminating in softening of the brain. In a lucid interval, on his birthday in February 1860, he said, "Christ is precious. I am not sorry I have preached Christ; but when my work is all done, I want to go home."

Joshua M. Chamberlain, son of Eli and Achsah Chamberlain, was born in 1825; was graduated at Dartmouth College in 1855, and at Andover Theological Seminary at 1858. Early in the following year he went to Dubuque, Iowa, and for a time supplied a pulpit in that city. In 1860 he became pastor of the Congregational Church in Des Moines, Iowa, from which relation he was, at his own request, dismissed in 1866. Since that time he has been agent for the American Missionary Association in the same State, and is, at present, engaged in collecting funds for Iowa College.

Edward Payson Thwing, son of Deacon Thomas and Grace (Barnes) Thwing, although not born until a few years after his father removed from this place, yet seems so thoroughly identified with us as to claim here a notice. He was born August 25, 1830 at Ware Village. In his seventh year he was a member of the primary department of West

Brookfield Academy, then under the charge of Mrs. C. P. F. Wheelock, afterward Mrs. Jesse Bliss. In November, 1837, he removed with his father's family to Boston, his father having entered upon his missionary labors in that city the previous January. It was at about this time, when he was seven years of age, that he gave his heart to Christ. Having studied at the Eliot Grammar School, and the High School of Boston, and two years at Monson Academy, he entered Harvard University, where he was graduated in 1855, and the summer of that year he spent in foreign travel. He was graduated at Andover Theological Seminary in 1858; having been licensed to preach by the Middlesex South Association in December 1857; was ordained pastor of the St. Lawrence Street Church, Portland, Maine, September 22, 1858, whence, after four and a half year's labor, he was released to accept a call to Quincy, (Massachusetts,) where he was installed November 19, 1862, and where he closed his pastoral connection on account of impaired health, July 1, 1867. He has published "Bible Sketches," (1854,) a small volume written while he was in college; "Leaves from a Tourist's Journal," a serial on foreign travel, in ten numbers, published in the Waverly Magazine, Boston; sermons—"Death of the First Born;" "Royal Request;" "A Voice from the Battle-field;" "Public Worship," and three other discourses which appeared in the Home Monthly, Boston, of which Mr. Thwing was editor for upwards of a year. Also a Biographical Sketch of Mrs. Grace W. Thwing, (1865,) and the "History of Beechwood Church," (1867.)

Leander T. Chamberlain, son of Eli and Achsah Chamberlain, was born in 1837, and was graduated at Yale College in 1863, with the highest honors of his class. After graduation he was, for three years, in the employ of the United States government, as paymaster in the navy, at Callao, South America, since which time he has been pursuing his theological studies at New Haven and Andover, and is now a member of the Seminary in the latter place.

SABBATH SCHOOL.

The Sabbath School dates its origin as early as 1817, when, through the agency of a few individuals, prominent among whom was Mr. Thomas Thwing,* classes were formed for the study of the Bible, in the interval of divine worship. At first these little groups met in private houses, and for a time, also, in a shop then standing near the house now occupied by Mrs. Otis Rawson. Subsequently they came together in the Old Center School-house. It was not till 1819 that the school assembled in this house, when classes were formed in the different pews, (which, at that time, were little square pens with seats on all sides,) and the affairs of the school began to be conducted in a more systematic way.

The exercises then consisted chiefly in the recitation of verses of Scripture, beginning with the first chapter of John. As an incentive to effort, the pupils were to try who would repeat the greatest number of verses. At the close of that season, a general meeting was held, and a sermon was preached by the pastor, Rev. Mr. Phelps, from the text in Deuteronomy 6 : 7—"*And thou shalt teach them diligently to thy children.*" The records of the school were also read; the

---

* Since deacon of the East Congregational Church, Ware, and for more than thirty years City Missionary in Boston. He died May 5, 1867, aged seventy-five.

number of verses which each scholar had committed was announced publicly, and the names of individuals who had committed the largest number were honorably mentioned.

The first item that appears upon our church records in relation to the Sabbath School, and showing a more complete organization, is dated May 4, 1821, when it was voted—"That Captain J. Smith, Deacon J. Ross, J. Hinshaw, Thomas Bond, Esq., Solomon Gilbert, Thomas Thwing, and Deacon A. White, be a Committee to take the oversight of the Sabbath School for the ensuing season." It was not till a yet later date that the first superintendent, Deacon Josiah Cary, was chosen.

For a number of years the school was continued only through the summer. In its earliest years, it encountered no little opposition. The whole system of Sabbath School instruction was then it its embryo. It was almost wholly a a new enterprise in this country, and this was the *first school* in this part of Massachusetts. A strong prejudice existed against it, and it commenced, as Doctor Phelps says, "with a load of odium upon it. The first that had been heard of the Sunday-School, was as a sort of *literary 'soup-house'* for the children of the poor, and for those only who lived in the large cities. Some efforts of the kind had been attempted in Boston. But it was not considered as adapted to the country villages at all." Several of the good Christian people of this place "were very much opposed to it, as a desecration of the Sabbath;" and it was not till after two or three seasons of successful operation "had shown to the people what the practical working of the thing was, that some even of the church would let their children attend." It has long since come to be a popular institution, looked upon as an almost indispensable auxiliary to the instructions of the family and the pulpit, and, in some sense, is regarded as *the hope of the Church.*

The Sunday School Concert, held on the second Sabbath evening of each month, is of comparatively recent origin, and is an exceedingly interesting feature of the school. During the present year the school has received a considerable accession to its numbers; and among them a *class of the recent converts*, composed of men most of whom are *past middle life*, so that the school now consists of three hundred and eleven members. And whereas at first the school had no books of any sort, other than the Bible, it now has not only the more modern appliances of question books, and singing-books, but also a choice library of five hundred and fifty volumes, a large portion of which are new.

MISSIONARIES AND MISSIONARY SPIRIT.

This church, during the last half century, has not been wanting in the Missionary spirit. It was among the very earliest in the country, and the *first* in this part of Massachusetts, to introduce the Monthly Missionary Concert, fifty-one years ago. This meeting was formerly held on the first Monday evening of each month; but for years past, has occurred, as at present, regularly on the first Sabbath evening of the month; and generally secures a large attendance.

In the year 1824, the Auxiliary Foreign Missionary Society of the Brookfield Association was formed in this place. Its annual meetings alternate among the several towns embraced within this Association, and occur on the third Tuesday after the first Monday in October of each year. Our yearly contributions to the American Board are made through this Auxiliary Society; and, from the time of its organization to the present year, our contributions for that object have amounted to six thousand and eighty-four dollars and nineteen cents.

In another place under the head of "*Ministers from the Church and Parish*," we speak of Rev. Messrs. Nichols and Spear, members of this church, as having labored on Home Missionary ground; and of Rev. William W. Howland as now successfully engaged in the Foreign field in Ceylon, where for the last twenty-two years, he has preached the Gospel to the inhabitants of that Island. But, besides these ordained Missionaries, this church has made yet other contributions of its members to that great work,—"*the healing of the nations*."

Daniel Chamberlain, son of Deacon Daniel and Lydia Chamberlain, removed to this town from Westborough in 1806; united with this church by profession in 1814; and was closely identified in 1819 with the *first mission* to the Sandwich Islands. Opukahaia (Obookiah) of the "Mission School" at Cornwall, Connecticut, had died the previous year; but he had not lived in vain. Though not himself permitted to return and preach the Gospel to his own countrymen, there had been awakened in the minds of others in this country an interest and sympathy which gave birth to the great enterprise of converting those Islands to God.

"In the summer of 1819, Hiram Bingham and Asa Thurston, students in the Theological Seminary at Andover, offered themselves to the American Board for this service. They were ordained at Goshen, Connecticut, September 19. Others offered themselves as assistant missionaries; a mission church was organized in the vestry of Park Street Church,

Boston, October 15. The public instructions of the Prudential Committee were given by the Secretary, Rev. Dr. Worcester, the same evening, and on the 23d of the same month, (October 1819,)—forty-eight years ago—the company sailed from Boston in the brig Thaddeus, Captain Blanchard," * and reached the Islands early in the following April. In this company there were as members of the mission seventeen persons, among whom, besides the ordained missionaries Bingham and Thurston, with their wives, there were three natives of the Islands, also a physician, a mechanic, a catechist, a printer, and a farmer. It was in this last capacity that Mr. Chamberlain went, accompanied by his wife and four children. After an absence of about five years he returned to this place, and soon after removed to Westborough where he died in February 1860,—the same year in which the American Board completed the first half century of its existence. He is remembered as a very ingenious man, a devoted Christian, and a most valuable member of society.

Miss Adaline White, daughter of Deacon Alfred and Sarah (Gilbert) White, was born September 25, 1809; united with this church March 4, 1827; sailed July 4, 1834 for Singapore, Siam, where she was married to Rev. Ira Tracy, January 15, 1835. On account of the feeble health of her husband, they returned to this country in August 1841. Four years later they removed to Streetsboro, Ohio, where she died March 3, 1851. Her only surviving child, Alfred Edwards Tracy, was born in West Brookfield, July 2, 1845, and is now in the Junior Class at Amherst College.

Miss Sarah G. White, daughter of Deacon Alfred and

---

* Newcomb's Cyclopedia of Missions, p. 649.

Sarah (Gilbert) White, was born September 14, 1813; united with this church May 3, 1835; was married to Rev. Asa B. Smith, March 15, 1838; and that same day set out on a mission to the Oregon Indians, going as far as New York by stage. From Fort Independence they started May 1, in company with the missionaries Messrs. Eells, Walker and Gray, and their wives, and on the last day of September reached Fort Vancouver, beyond the Rocky Mountains, then in Western Oregon, but now embraced within the limits of Washington Territory. They made this long tedious journey on horseback, escorted by Indian fur traders. Much of the time they were surrounded by hostile Indians, and were compelled to endure great hardships. Having spent a few years in missionary labor among the Indians of Oregon, they went thence to the Sandwich Islands Mission; where they labored some two or three years, and then, by reason of Mr. Smith's failing health, they returned by way of China, reaching home in 1846. They brought with them three children, daughters of Mr. Locke of the Sandwich Islands Mission, the two eldest of whom were adopted by Mr. Smith, and the youngest by an uncle. The eldest is now married to Rev. Elijah Harmon. About two years after their return, Mrs. Smith removed with her husband to Buckland, Massachusetts, where she died May 27, 1855.

The name of Rev. Samuel Ware Bonney appears also upon our Catalogue as having united with the church May 7, 1837, and as having been dismissed soon after to Danbury, Connecticut. There is, however, some reason to question whether he ever belonged to this church. His widowed mother resided here for a few years, and was a member of this church about two years and a half, from July, 1845, to December,

1847. But there seems to be no certain evidence that her son was ever connected with us. A word respecting him, however, may not be out of place. He was a son of Rev. William and Mrs. Sarah (Ware) Bonney; was born in New Canaan, Connecticut, in 1815; in 1832 he was in the employment of the Messrs. Merriam, publishers, at Springfield, (Massachusetts.) In 1837 he was engaged in teaching at Poughkeepsie, New York. He afterwards studied at the New York University, and at Lane Seminary, Ohio; received an appointment as missionary of the American Board, and in 1846 began his labors at Canton, China, where he continued to labor with great devotion and self-denial, and with marked success, until his death, which occurred July 27, 1864. At a meeting of the Canton Missionary Conference, held on the third of the succeeding month, the following among other resolutions, was adopted:—

"That while we mourn our loss, it is felt that the life and death of our brother gave abundant cause for thankfulness to our Lord and Saviour, for the grace given him, in the fulfillment of his ministry, and in his dying testimony."

PATRIOTISM.

I should seem to depreciate the value of our free institutions and republican government as connected with the progress of Christ's Kingdom in our land and world, and to be strangely unmindful of the noble part which the Christian Church has performed in the preservation of those inestimable blessings, particularly in the recent mighty civil conflict of the nation, did I not in closing, at least barely mention the well know and tried patriotism of this church and people, as an important additional element of their wide and beneficent influence.

In May 1776, two months previous to the Declaration of Independence, the inhabitants of this town pledged their almost unanimous support to the Continental Congress if they should see fit to declare the colonies independent of Great Britain; and during the entire war of the Revolution, they did not fail to redeem their pledge. And the man who through that whole period, was foremost in the deliberations and acts of the town, as in loyalty to his country, was the Hon. Jedediah Foster, a deacon in this church. But especially during these late years of peril, disaster and bloodshed, there has been no backward response to the urgent calls of the country, either on the part of our church or community, whether in men or money, whether in clothing for the destitute, or food for the hungry, or in timely ministrations to the sick, the wounded and the dying. Our hand, moreover, is even now wide open to welcome the long oppressed to the rights and privileges of citizens, and, at the same time, generously to dispense to the needy among them of our kindly Christian charities.

Whether in time of war or of peace, we are solemnly bound to be true to the instincts of patriotism and philanthropy, and to the higher promptings of our religious faith.

Such is an imperfect review of our long and not uneventful history. From this summary of the events of a century and a half, we find that whatever may be the sources of regret as we revert to the past on this Anniversary Day, they are far outnumbered and outweighed by the many occasions for joy and devoutest thanksgiving to God.

This ancient Church has had its severe, though brief, trial seasons, its short-lived days of darkness and sterility; but it has also had its long and happy periods of prosperity and abundant fruitfulness. Like the veteran soldier, not without wounds and scars has it fought its battles and won its victories. But these visible marks of violence only make the more clearly manifest that merciful and marvelous interposition by which the Church has been preserved. To one baptism of suffering, God has sent a score of the joyful baptisms of the Holy Ghost; so that the hearts of hundreds have here been made to leap for joy, and their tongues loosed in the praise of redeeming grace.

A precious, sacred trust is this, and exalted, blessed privileges these, which our pious fathers have so carefully perpetuated and handed down to us. But in proportion to the greatness and sacredness of the blessings we have inherited from the past, so great and solemn is our obligation to cherish those blessings in our own day, and to deliver them over in all their fulness to coming generations.

In view of our numerous past and present mercies, OUR RESPONSIBILITY INDEED IS GREAT. From the heights of these one hundred and fifty years of Gospel privilege the eyes of five generations of godly men look down upon us. And upon their lips to-day is the question, well-nigh solemn as the eternity to which they are now mostly gone, "Will you transmit unimpaired to posterity this noble heritage, which, through much hard toil, and many tears and prayers, we have committed to you?"

Yea, rather, from the bosom of eternity itself, there seems to fall upon our ear at this memorable hour, in accents of heavenly earnestness, the united voice of the hundreds whose feet have reverently trod these earthly courts, but who now walk the golden streets, saying, "Watch ye, stand fast in the faith, quit you like men, be strong." "Earnestly contend for the faith which was once delivered unto the saints." "Love this dear old Church of Christ unto the end. Stand by her in the time of her trial. Seek her purity, her peace, her prosperity, her continual growth. Pray that she may keep her garments unsullied, her name without reproach, not in the present merely, but down through the years and centuries to come, until at last the Bridegroom shall 'present it to himself a glorious church, not having spot, or wrinkle, or any such thing.'"

Poem.

MEMORIALS OF BROOKFIELD,

BY REV. FRANCIS HORTON, OF BARRINGTON, R. I.

ANALYSIS. — Invocation and Gratulation — Scenery and Associations — Scenery still, and Cultivation, and Children — The Village, with its Walks, its Sanctuary and Sabbaths — Moral and Industrial Habits of Society — Favorable and Beautiful Surroundings — Former Residents and Local Attachments — Historic Reflections, Education, etc. — Religious Usages — Excellence of Domestic Character and Training — Worthy Ancestors and Ministers — Success of the Present Pastor — Historic Incidents, Revivals, and their Influence, especially the Last — Afflictions, Various and Personal — Fraternal Greetings — Anticipations, and Prayer for Posterity.

God of eternity, whose power
  Preserves us, and our fathers blest,
Be with us at this hallowed hour,
  And let us in Thy presence rest.
Here would we come with praise and prayer,
  Thy gracious goodness to confess,
Whose favor children's children share,
  In trust Thou wilt our offspring bless.
As pilgrims to a holy shrine,
  We gather joyously to greet
Each other, as in olden time,
  Thrice happy thus once more to meet.

A festival is this of years,
  A jubilee of grateful kind,
Where minglings of smiles and tears
  Refresh the heaven-aspiring mind.
No vain regrets or glooms we bring,
  No sad remembrances of strife,
But rather one glad offering
  To Him who is our spirit's life.
His may we be, a blessed band
  Of brotherhood by heavenly birth,
All journeying to the better land
  Whose paradise is not of earth.

Still cherish we this favored scene
  Of toils, and friendships, griefs, and joys,
Though brighter visions intervene,
  Of bliss that hath no dark alloys.
Fond memories of the past we trace,
  'Mid plains, and hills, and sculptured stones,
And trees that with their grandeur grace
  These sacred sites, and dear old homes.
Yon river, gentle as of yore,
  Glides peacefully towards the sea,
Repeating fondly o'er and o'er
  Sweet strains of Nature's minstrelsy.
Nor less the birds that flit above,
  Or skim the surface of that stream,
In warbling tones of truth and love,
  Gladden the meadows fresh and green.
Yon lakelet in its beauty lies
  As when our fathers dwelt around—
A molten mirror of the skies—
  How clear, how tranquil, how profound!

Look thither, at the twilight hour,
  The sunset or the moonlight scene,
And feel the pacifying power
  Alluring to the world unseen.
There gaze upon the vault of night,
  Whence stars look down on shadows here,
Discoursing of those realms of light
  That canopy our dusky sphere.
What wondrous influences blend,
  To bless the soul on heaven intent;
And pilgrims on the earth befriend
  With sweet provisions for content.

Each hillside sloping towards the plain,
  Has sightly homesteads nestling there,
With garden spots, and fields of grain,
  And ripened fruits, all fresh and fair;
And chubby children issuing thence,
  In quest of berries or of flowers,
Blest samples of fair innocence,
  Enjoy the glad autumnal hours.
Goodness! what glories flood the fields,
  Where lawns, and groves, and orchards lie,
And every acre somehow yields
  Its affluence 'neath the sunny sky!
Whose is the heart that does not rise
  In gratitude to God above,
Whose favor and whose grace supplies
  Such proofs of His paternal love?

Then look again—the village green
  Smiles cheerfully the church around,
While numerous shops and dwellings seen,

Say thrift, and skill, and taste abound.
The shaded walks across the plain,
Broad avenues beside, well trod,
Are traveled not alone for gain—
All leading to the house of God.
Thither assemblies oft convene,
For praise, and preaching, and for prayer,
Where generations past have been,
In search of heavenly guidance there.
Glad voices greet the day of rest;
Hearts weary with their worldly care,
Or sorrow-stricken and distressed,
To Zion's altars here repair.
The Comforter, the Paraclete,
Whose office is to heal the soul,
Thus meets men at the mercy-seat,
Willing and waiting to make whole.
O what a balm the Sabbath brings,
To spirits seeking fresh supplies
Of holy influence at these springs,
Whose source is found in Paradise!

The week day world is tranquil here—
Of riot and of ranting void;
Nor child nor matron need e'er fear
With violence to be annoyed;
Save such excess as sin and crime
May bring to any spot of earth,
Where baser passions in their time
Incontinently spring to birth.
What industries are well supplied;
What habits savoring of health;
Not nursing indolence, or pride,

Yet nourishing the common wealth!
No ministries to public vice,
Destructive of the social weal,
Or schemes of crushing avarice,
The doings of the day reveal.
Thus labor hath its recompense,
Work of the lusty brawn or brain,
And all have healthful competence,
The landlord, and the humblest swain.

Extend the view, on either side,
Which trade or travel may incline,
And see the prospect opening wide,
No artist's pencil can define;
The hills ascend—their summits climb—
And gaze around where'er you stand;
Observe what elements combine
To beautify and bless the land!
Each sunny slope, and graceful swell,
Each pasture, with its lowing herd,
Each rivulet, and mossy well,
Salutes you with a welcome word:
"Pause, pilgrim, and enjoy the sight;
Communion hold with Nature here,
Drink in the fullness of delight,
Which dignifies this earthly sphere;
Nor deem it strange that those who trod
These paths aforetime, in their prime,
Held converse with Almighty God,
'Mid flush of scenery so smblime!"

Yet where are they—the stalwart men—
That traversed thus these hills and plains?

Whose like we ne'er may see again,
  Save as posterity remains;
And worthy women, meek in mein,
  Of aspect and of movement bland,
What wives and mothers then were seen,
  The joy and glory of the land!
Daughters of Brookfield, ever fair;
  With health and energy endowed,
Domestic jewelry most rare,
  Of which the dwelling may be proud.
Sisters and sons, with grateful sires,
  The labors of the homestead share,
While neither to the fame aspires
  Of uselessness or ennui there.
All love the country — well they may;
  Its atmosphere, its trees, its fields,
The summer and the spring so gay,
  And golden fruits that autumn yields.
Here winter hath its hearty joys,
  With books, and friends, and music blest,
While each his industry employs
  To render happy all the rest.

Thrice fifty years their course have run,
  Eventful in their various date,
Since godly fathers here begun
  The history we commemorate.
Scarce had fierce savages retired
  From streams and grounds they loved so well,
When friendly spirits prompt aspired
  In Christian fellowship to dwell.
No respite to their toils and cares,
  Would those heroic men afford,

Nor ceasing from their alms and prayers,
  Unitedly to serve the Lord—
Till place was found for worship free,
  Amid these pleasant vales and woods;
Provision for society,
  Instead of wastes and solitudes.
Honor to those who sought to lay
  Foundations for religion pure,
And to posterity convey
  A heritage of good so sure.

Their culture of the mind, no less
  Than ground that needed earnest toil,
To rescue from the wilderness,
  And render it a fruitful soil,
Secured at once most constant care,
  And steady exercise of skill,
The harvest wealth of soul to share,
  Which was their wisdom and their will.
Thus, near the church the school-house rose,
  However humble, still at hand;
As with religion learning goes,
  Enriching liberally the land.
E'en then what sportive games were seen,
  When children sprightly, fresh, and fair,
Tripped gaily o'er the village green,
  With guileless face, and flowing hair.
The spelling-book was not forgot,
  Nor Testament perchance, though rare,
As issued from their humble cot
  The little groups so free from care,
To meet the Mistress of the day,
  Whose smile was sure, whose word was rule,

Who favored knowledge more than play,
  Within her well-taught, simple school.
True, John was roguish now and then,
  And James too restless to sit still,
And Mary missed her page or pen,
  [Now obsolete the gray goose-quill.]
Some stolen glances, too, were paid—
  Ever, of course, against the rule—
From loving youth to blushing maid,
  The merest accident at school;
Still study was the main pursuit,
  Good learning and good manners taught,
"The young idea how to shoot,"
  Was foremost in the teacher's thought.
Slight rivalries perhaps arise,
  As pupils on success intent
The head to keep, and win the prize,
  Nor suffer social detriment.
These have their stimulus, to aid
  The indolent in quest of lore,
Inspiring those of various grade,
  To lessons never learned before.
Fond intimacies ere long grow
  To richer ripeness in the heart,
Till schoolmates are constrained to show
  Reluctance evermore to part.
These signify their several choice,
  In tokens never meaningless,
Each causing other to rejoice
  In wedlock sure their lives to bless.
The nuptials finally are sealed,
  With fitting rites and general glee,
And friendly feelings are revealed

In generous hospitality.
Thus families arise and spread—
Society its ranks extends—
Though fond ones drop among the dead,
The fairest and the best of friends!

Yet other strains our theme requires:
Time runs too rapidly to waste;
And we are following our sires,
In paths no more to be retraced.
They had their Sabbaths, blessed days,
And sermons from the wise and good,
Sweet seasons oft of prayer and praise,
When worldlings dared not intrude.
So had they sacraments of grace,
Such as their children still sustain,
The sacred font, in time and place,
Serving the covenant the same;
Symbol of cleansing and of cure,
Pure water sprinkled on the brow,
Doth all of simple form insure,
Availing to the service now.
Christ's table spread with bread and wine,
Choice elements, expressive still,
Perpetuates the feast divine
Of those who seek to do his will.
What numbers here have followed him,
Obedient to his blest command,
Whose spirits pure have entered in,
And joined the bright celestial band.
There dwell they with the sainted host,
Whose song on earth was wont to rise
To Father, Son, and Holy Ghost,
Jehovah great, above the skies!

Those holy men who trod these ways,
  In paths of pleasantness and peace,
Whose memory we rightly praise,
  Whose influence will never cease—
Well bore the burden of their day,
  Working with all their might and main,
Foundations here in truth to lay,
  The cause of virtue to sustain.
What care had they to leave behind,
  Not lands alone, and dwellings good,
But nurture for the immortal mind,
  Substantial spiritual food!
Such training children had in course,
  From saintly mothers and from sires,
As told the nature and the source
  Of their intense and kind desires.
Born of the Spirit from above,
  And blest with teachings so divine,
It was the prompting of pure love,
  To let their bright example shine.
How intimate with Heaven were they;
  How conversant with sacred truth,
Which was their study day by day,
  The rule of life, the guide of youth.
Happy those homes whence daily prayer,
  In grateful offering arose
To Him whose tender mercies spare,
  And give at night serene repose.
What favored families were theirs,
  Whose parentage was so replete
With blessings for themselves and heirs,
  Forth flowing from the mercy-seat.

Ancestral honors well we prize,
  And social benefits no less,
From "parents passed into the skies,"
  Who wrought such works of righteousness.
Preachers besides, for scores of years,
  Glad tidings here of grace proclaimed,
With weary watchings, toils and tears,
  Of whom we need not be ashamed.
Successive pastors reverence claim,
  Who fed this flock in days of yore,
Whose record is enduring fame,
  To live when time shall be no more.
One still survives, whose hoary head*
  It gladdens us afresh to see,
Though most are numbered with the dead,
  Who waited on his ministry.
His is the privilege to wait
  A little longer on these shores,
Ere passing to that higher state,
  Where is the Lamb whom he adores.
Others there are who since have stood
  On Zion's walls as watchmen here,
Whose influence, however good,
  It may not be their choice to hear.
These severally have sought to know
  Their high commission from above,
And clearly to the people show
  The riches of eternal love.
Of God—of man—of Christ—of heaven,
  They taught right tenderly, and true;
The way to have our sins forgiven,

---

* Rev. Eliakim Phelps, D. D.

And to begin our lives anew.
Ah, well they harmonized in this,
What every human soul must be,
To enter through the gates of bliss,
And dwell with God eternally.
Nor less do they in heart rejoice
At Zion's increase and success,
Praying with one consent and voice,
That God will still his servant bless.
This latest leader* may he crown
With glory's signal coronet,
When he shall lay his armor down,
With trophies at our Savior's feet.
Historic incidents we trace,
In scenes of joyance and of grief,
As blessings have enriched the place,
Or trials called for large relief.
Seasons of grace have been enjoyed,
In measure more than we can tell,
When God and men have been employed
In saving sinful souls from hell.
The spirit hovering around,
Has startled slumberers to think,
And made them hear the dreadful sound,
As standing on that fatal brink,
Whence fierce destruction flashes wrath,
And echoes vengeance at each breath,
Sweeping the guilty mortal's path
With warnings of eternal death!
Anon there comes a welcome voice,
Winning the trembling heart to rest,

---

* Rev. Samuel Dunham.

And bids it make the happy choice,
And be with grace and glory blest.
What looks of loveliness has He
Who agonized for human guilt,
And hung upon that cursed tree,
Where blood, most precious blood was spilt!
Was it for us he bled and died—
The harmless sufferer for sin—
The Son of God thus crucified
That we might endless glory win!
Then dearest service evermore,
Submission sweet, and faith, and love,
Are due to Jesus o'er and o'er,
In realms below, and realms above!
All praise to that eternal plan
Which Sovereign Goodness saw and chose,
By which to save rebellious man,
And reconcile malicious foes!
Strains such as these have often rung,
From many ransomed souls forgiven,
Whose offerings of the heart and tongue,
Have raised their incense pure to heaven.

O happy hours of praise and prayer,
When converts from the world have come
Like little children, to declare,
What love divine for them hath done!
Their tongues are loosed, their lips unsealed,
Their hearts with gratitude o'erflow;
The blessedness to be revealed,
Is such as only Christians know.
These have their sympathies expressed,
In joys the stranger feeleth not,

Or anxiousness for souls distressed,
  Once felt, not easily forgot.
Yet harvest times have often come,
  Ingatherings of goodly grain,
To this our temporary home,
  So recently refreshed again.
Thanks to the Lord whose loving power,
  The blessing in advance has sent
To consecrate this festive hour
  As one of mutual content.
Third jubilee of years—how blest!
  The period we celebrate,
Is worthily the pilgrim's rest,
  In prospect of a purer state.

Let not our lyre refuse a strain
  Of plaintive melody the while,
Though little more of time remain
  Than friendly parting with a smile.
While Providence hath largely blest
  Our various residences here,
It hath not been unbroken rest,
  Void of affliction, or of fear.
No—clouds have come o'er brightest skies,
  And sorrow visited each heart;
Grave memories of grief arise,
  In which we shared a mourner's part.
What shadows have each threshold crossed,
  Where sunlight had been bright before;
What treasures have our dwellings lost,
  That nought on earth can e'er restore.
Parents and children have been borne
  In turn to yonder sacred spot,

Leaving more lonely ones to mourn
  Sad vacancies not soon forgot.
Sisters and brothers too, how fond,
  Have separated at the grave,
Not solaced with a thought beyond,
  But the Redeemer's power to save.
Others more dear have gone the way
  Whence no returning footsteps come;
And widowed mourners see no day
  When seems it as before at home.
How many mingle thus their tears,
  O'er sorrows which each heart can feel,
That e'en the silent lapse of years
  Has no effective power to heal!

The youngest from the cradle dear,
  How sadly is it laid aside
In that receptacle so drear,
  Where many of its class abide.
Yet few the families exempt
  From sorrow over children fled,
And silencing of merriment,
  That such are numbered with the dead.
Forgive the strain, the gentle sigh,
  Parental fondness, if you please,
That brings some moisture to the eye,
  In sympathy with scenes like these.
Three little graves are side by side,
  In yon inclosure near the gate,
With tablets severally supplied
  To mark the name, the age, the date:
A sister and two brothers there,
  Sleep peacefully beneath the sod,

In after ages to appear
  Among the risen saints of God.
Our infant offspring, why deplore,
  When suddenly removed from sight?
Faith says, "Not lost, but gone before,"
  To regions of celestial light.
Thither let us henceforth aspire,
  With purer ardor for the prize,
All cherishing devout desire
  To dwell with them above the skies.

Fraternal greetings we exchange
  With friendly spirits here at home,
Ingathered from an ample range,
  Whence various duty calls to roam.
This mother church her children dear
  Invites beneath the old rooftree,
Together thus their hearts to cheer,
  And bind in bonds of charity.
Daughters of comeliness and strength,
  Surround her here on every hand,
Whose goodly influence at length
  Extends, how widely in the land!
E'en foreign shores are sometimes trod
  By those who go far hence to teach
The lively oracles of God,
  And his incarnate love to preach.
Welcome, right welcome, all who come
  To celebrate this festal day,
Which calls a mother's children home,
  Their grateful offerings to pay.
Yes, welcome all to this repast,
  So rich in sacred memories

Well gathered from the fruitful past,
  To give us plenteous supplies.
Here let the hand, the heart, the voice,
  Their friendly sentiments express,
And each in other's joy rejoice,
  With pure unbounded thankfulness.
Thus as the moments glide apace,
  As moves the Autumn's golden sun,
No cloud shall cross our cheerful face,
  Till day's delightful work is done.

What though as now no more we meet,
  To take such retrospect of time—
Or gather round this sacred seat,
  Where memories so sweet combine?
A larger company ere long
  Will greet us on the shining shore,
And join in one triumphant song,
  That there we meet to part no more!
All hail the prospect, ever bright,
  Of meeting in that world above,
Where all is purity and light;
  All righteousness, and peace, and love!
Still would we breathe a fervent prayer,
  That those who follow in our train
May evermore most largely share
  These priceless blessings that remain.
May children's children here enjoy
  Rich benefits of Gospel grace,
And mightiest energies employ
  To renovate and save the race.
Thus may the blest succession run,
  In ages future as the past;

Nay, brighter, like the shining sun,
  Each generation till the last.
Then come with joy each golden year,
  To celebrate this jubilee,
Till nations shout the triumph here,
  Which earth has sighed so long to see!

Appendix.

ORDER OF PROCEEDINGS.

At a meeting of the Congregational Church in West Brookfield, Massachusetts, held at the conclusion of the preparatory lecture, Friday afternoon, July 5, 1867, it was voted to celebrate the One Hundred and Fiftieth Anniversary of the formation of the Church, to occur on Wednesday the sixteenth day of the succeeding October; and at the same time the following persons were chosen a Committee to make all necessary arrangements for the occasion, viz:

Avery Keep,	John M. Fales,*
Abner C. Gleason,	Raymond Cummings,
Rev. Samuel Dunham,	Warren A. Blair,
Dea. Moses Hall,	Charles E. Smith,
Adolphus Hamilton,	Dea. Alfred White,

Sherlock D. Livermore.

In the evening of the day on which the above Committee were chosen, they met, and organized by the choice of Rev. S. Dunham, chairman. and S. D. Livermore, secretary, and voted to submit the whole matter of the arrangements to the consideration of a sub-committee of three, who should report at a future meeting. Messrs. Dunham, Gleason, and Hall were appointed to that service.

The Committee subsequently met and voted that the pastor be invited to deliver an Historical Discourse, and to procure the writing of an Anniversary Hymn, and a Poem.

*Died suddenly of heart disease Friday morning after the Anniversary, October 18, 1867.

They also issued a circular letter, inviting former Pastors, Ministers reared in the parish, Members and Friends of the Church generally, to be present and participate in the exercises of the celebration.

They further determined to have a general collation, and chose a Committee on Collation, consisting of the following named gentlemen:

Edward T. Stowell,	Dea. Samuel N. White,
William Paige,	William Adams, Jr.,
Joseph E. Bailey,	Warren A. Blair,
Curtis Gilbert,	Lyman H. Chamberlain.

The Committee of Arrangements likewise elected John M. Fales a Committee on Finance; appointed the officers of the day, and prepared the order of exercises.

The Celebration fell upon the delightful season of Indian Summer, and proved to be one of Nature's balmiest days. The occasion drew together a large assembly from a wide region of country, and perhaps exceeded in interest and enjoyment the expectations even of the most sanguine.

OFFICERS OF THE DAY.

PRESIDENT,

Rev. FRANCIS HORTON.

VICE PRESIDENTS,

Dea. GEORGE MERRIAM,	Rev. ELIAKIM PHELPS, D. D.,
Dea. JACOB DUPEE,	ADOLPHUS HAMILTON, Esq.,

Dea. ALFRED WHITE.

COMMITTEE OF RECEPTION,

S. D. LIVERMORE, A. C. GLEASON,

C. E. SMITH.

CHIEF MARSHAL,

HARRISON BARNES.

ASSISTANT MARSHALS,

EBENEZER B. LYNDE,	GEORGE W. BILSS,
LEWIS GLEASON,	JOSEPH S. GLEASON,
IRA M. SOUTHWORTH,	GEORGE W. STONE.

ORDER OF EXERCISES.

MORNING.

VOLUNTARY—ANTHEM.

Tune—Denmark.

Before Jehovah's awful throne,
  Ye nations, bow with sacred joy:
Know that the Lord is God alone;
  He can create, and he destroy.

His sovereign power, without our aid,
  Made us of clay, and formed us men;
And when, like wand'ring sheep, we strayed,
  He brought us to his fold again.

We are his people, we his care,
  Our souls, and all our mortal frame:
What lasting honors shall we rear,
  Almighty Maker, to thy name?

We'll crowd thy gates with thankful songs,
  High as the heaven our voices raise;
And earth, with her ten thousand tongues,
  Shall fill thy courts with sounding praise.

Wide as the word is thy command,
  Vast as eternity, thy love:
Firm as a rock thy truth shall stand,
  When rolling years shall cease to move.

INVOCATION AND READING OF THE SCRIPTURES, by Rev. Joshua Coit, of Brookfield.

SINGING.

Heavenly Father, graciously hear us;
  Hear the petitions we offer before Thee;
Let thy mercy rest upon us;
  Heavenly Father, graciously hear us;
    Hear our prayer, Hear our prayer.

PRAYER, by Rev. L. S. Parker, of Derry, New Hampshire.

Anniversary Hymn.

[Words by Miss Carrie A. Parker, of Derry, New Hampshire.]

Tune—Dedham.

Thrice fifty years have swiftly flown,
  Since first a little band
Of Christian laborers set this vine,
  And trained with loving hand.

The Lord hath visited His vine
  With showers of heavenly grace,
And blessed His waiting children's eyes
  With shining of His face.

The precious seed in weakness sown,
  And watered well with tears,
Hath grown unto a noble tree,
  And generous fruitage bears.

While humble souls have watched and prayed,
  And with temptation fought,
God hath made bare his own right arm,
  And great deliverance brought.

His hand hath loosed the captive's bonds,
  He bade the slave go free;
His voice the heathen nations calls
  To Christian liberty.

And now his still, small voice is heard
  Through our redeemed land:
"Go, Christians, in my vineyard work,
  Nor longer idle stand."

Not the anointed ones alone,
  As preachers, now are sent;
But all whose hearts have felt His love,
  And wills to His have bent.

Instead of sires, the children stand;
  To us may grace be given
To follow them in faithfulness,
  And share their joy in Heaven.

Historical Discourse, (in part,) by Rev. S. Dunham.

HYMN.

Tune—Harvard.

No change of time shall ever shock
  My trust, O Lord, in thee;
For thou hast always been my Rock,
  A sure defence to me.

Thou my deliv'rer art, O God;
  My trust is in thy power:
Thou art my shield from foes abroad,
  My safeguard, and my tower.

BENEDICTION, by Rev. Dr. Phelps.

RECESS—COLLATION.

AFTERNOON.

HYMN—THE CHURCH'S WELCOME.

Children of Zion! what harp-notes are stealing,
  So soft o'er our senses, so soothingly sweet?
'Tis the music of angels, their raptures revealing,
  That you have been bro't to the Holy One's feet.
Children of Zion! we join in their welcome,
  'Tis sweet to lie low at that blessed retreat.

Children of Zion! no longer in sadness,
  Refrain from the feast that your Savior hath given;
Come, taste of the cup of salvation with gladness,
  And think of the banquet still sweeter in heaven.
Children of Zion! our hearts bid you welcome
  To the church of the ransomed, the kingdom of heaven.

Children of Zion! we joyfully hail you,
  Who've entered the sheep-fold thro' Jesus, the door;
While pilgrims on earth, tho' the foe may assail you,
  Press forward, and soon will the conflict be o'er.
Children of Zion! Oh! welcome, thrice welcome!
  Till we meet where the foe shall oppress you no more.

HISTORICAL PAPERS: The Deacons and Meeting-Houses, by Rev. S. Dunham.

Hymn.

Tune—Olmutz.

Far down the ages now,
Much of her journey done,
The pilgrim church pursues her way,
Until her crown be won.

The story of the past
Come up before her view;
How will it seem to suit her still—
Old, and yet ever new!

It is the oft-told tale
Of sin and weariness,
Of grace and love yet flowing down
To pardon and to bless.

No wider is the gate,
No broader is the way,
No smoother is the ancient path,
That leads to life and day.

No sweeter is the cup,
Nor less our lot of ill:
'Twas tribulation ages since,
'Tis tribulation still.

No slacker grows the fight,
No feebler is the foe,
Nor less the need of armor tried,
Of shield and spear and bow.

Thus onward still we press
Through evil and through good,—
Through pain and poverty and want,
Through peril and through blood.

Still faithful to our God,
And to our Captain true,
We follow where he leads the way,
The kingdom in our view.

Address, by Rev. Eliakim Phelps, D. D., of Jersey City, New Jersey.

Remarks, by Rev. L. S. Parker, of Derry, New Hampshire.

Historical Sketch: Ministers from the Church and Parish, by Rev. S. Dunham.

Hymn.

Tune—Coronation.

Oh! 'twas a joyful sound to hear
 Our tribes devoutly say:
"Up, Israel, to the temple haste,
 And keep your festal day!"

At Salem's courts we must appear,
 With our assembled powers,
In strong and beauteous order ranged,
 Like her united towers.

Oh, pray we then for Salem's peace!
 For they shall prosperous be,
Thou holy city of our God,
 Who bear true love to thee.

May peace within thy sacred walls
 A constant guest be found;
With plenty and prosperity
 Thy palaces be crowned.

Poem: Memorials of Brookfield, by Rev. F. Horton, of Barrington, Rhode Island.

Remarks, by Hon. Amasa Walker, of North Brookfield.

Prayer, by Rev. William B. Bond, of Palmer.

Hymn.

Tune—Dismission.

Lord, dismiss us with thy blessing,
 Bid us all depart in peace;
Still on gospel manna feeding,
 Pure, seraphic love increase;
Fill each breast with consolation,
 Up to thee our voices raise;
When we reach that blissful station,
 Then we'll give thee noble praise.
  And we'll sing Hallelujah,
  To God and the Lamb;
  Hallelujah forever,—Amen.

Benediction, by Rev. Mr. Horton.

THE COLLATION.

Through the efficient exertions of the Committee who were entrusted with the task of providing the entertainment, this part of the day's exercises was rendered a complete success.

Previous to the day, this Committee appointed and made skillful disposition of the following ample corps of assistants, to superintend and aid in the distribution of the refreshments, viz:—

Anson Giffin Jr., Mrs. E. B. Taintor, Mrs. W. A. Marcy, Mrs. Sanford Adams, Mrs. B. P. Aikin, Mrs. Doct. Blodgett, Mrs. Doct. Forbes, Mrs. L. H. Chamberlain, Mrs. M. J. Miller, Mrs. Sarah J. Rawson, Mrs. G. W. Bliss, Mrs. Enos Gilbert, Mrs. W. A. Blair, Misses Abbie C. Blackmer, Eugenia Taintor, Ella G. Paige, Maria Reed, Ida E. Reed, Laura A. Giddings, Ida R. Giddings, Emma Rawson, Emma Sprout, Nettie Jackson, Clara J. Dane, Susie Beaman, Carrie M. Gleason, Annie Brown, Ann Elizabeth C. Gleason, Lottie M. White, Anna E. Bruce, Mary Jones, Julia Mirick, Lottie Miller, Arvilla Stone, Alice A. Richards, Messrs. Eddie F. Livermore, Alfred C. White, Frank L. Bailey, Alvin W. Gilbert, Augustus N. Makepeace, Charles S. Southworth, Albert W. Bliss.

At the close of the morning services, all who were present were invited to repair to the Town Hall, where a plentiful supply of provisions, of divers sorts, was in readiness, having being brought, by previous request, from every quarter of the town. The large audience was marshaled at the church, and proceeded to the hall in the following order:—Committee of Arrangements; President and Officers of the day; Clergy and Invited Guests; Strangers and Citizens generally.

The blessing having been invoked by Dr. Phelps, the appeals of hunger were sated by a repast which, as the Worcester Daily Spy of the next morning said, "was bountifully sufficient, good and well arranged, and set forth to the satisfaction of all who were privileged to partake."

At a meeting of the Church, held November 1, 1867, it was voted that measures be taken for publishing the doings of the anniversary celebration, and the following persons were appointed a Committee on publication:—A. C. Gleason, S. D. Livermore, Dea. J. Dupee, Rev. S. Dunham, W. A. Blair.

This Committee subsequently met, and by vote requested Rev. S.

Dunham to prepare an Appendix for the press, and authorized him to take the general superintendence of the publication.

LETTER FROM GOVERNOR BULLOCK.

COMMONWEALTH OF MASSACHUSETTS, EXECUTIVE DEPARTMENT, BOSTON, October 14, 1867.

My Dear Sir:—I am disappointed in failing to make my engagements such as to permit me to visit you on Wednesday. The One Hundred and Fiftieth Anniversary of the organization of your church is of itself a most interesting event even in a Commonwealth which we are accustomed to call ancient. Added to this is the equal interest attached to the old town of Brookfield which was for so many years scarcely second in political importance in the County of Worcester.

The town and the church in their historical relations cannot easily be separated; and it becomes to me a source of unfeigned regret that I cannot unite with you in commemorating the striking reminiscences which upon the present occasion will be awakened.

I am, my Dear Sir, with great respect and esteem,
Most truly, your obedient servant,
ALEX. H. BULLOCK.

THE REV. SAMUEL DUNHAM.

LETTER FROM REV. AUSTIN PHELPS, D. D., PROFESSOR IN THE THEOLOGICAL SEMINARY AT ANDOVER.

ANDOVER, Mass., September 18, 1867.

REV. S. DUNHAM: Dear Brother:—I am sorry that I cannot attend the Celebration at West Brookfield, but the state of my health puts it out of my power. My father, I think, will be there, and would doubtless be ready to fill any gap, should such a thing occur,—which is not probable. Your chief concern probably will be to stop the talkers.

I would, with great pleasure, be present, and speak just five minutes, watch in hand,—if my health would permit me to go.

Very truly yours, AUSTIN PHELPS.

LETTER FROM REV. CALEB SPRAGUE HENRY, D. D., OF NEWBURGH, NEW YORK.

NEWBURGH, N. Y., October, 14, 1867.

My Dear Sir:—Your kind invitation to the Celebration of the One Hundred and Fiftieth Anniversary of the organization of the Congregational Church in West Brookfield reached me in due season, but got mislaid until to-day I found it. I had meantime forgotten the day fixed for the festival; and now I perceive it is so near at hand that I am afraid this will not reach you before the day. I am the more sorry because events have occurred which will render it impossible for me to be present. It would give me great, very great pleasure to be there on the occasion. It is the church of my early childhood. The venerable image of Father Ward is one of the liveliest recollections of my childish days,—his white wig, his benignant face, his exquisite courtesy.

It was in that old white building on the north side of "the plain" that I first went to the Holy Communion. Of that church my venerable father was for many years a member. In the burial ground lies the body of my mother, and I suppose, of many more whom I once knew.

All these and many other associations with West Brookfield, would make it very pleasant for me to visit the place. I am sorry I cannot do so now. I live in the hope of doing so yet at some future day.

Very truly and respectfully yours, C. S. HENRY.

S. D. Livermore.

EXTRACT OF A LETTER FROM REV. JOSEPH VAILL, D. D., OF PALMER.

Palmer, September 20, 1867.

Dear Brother Dunham:—You allude to the anticipated Anniversary. It would give me great pleasure to be present, and I shall make an effort to do so. A special adjourned meeting of the Corporation of Amherst College is to take place about that time. If it does not occur on that week, I know of no obstacle to prevent my attendance.

I am truly and fatornally yours, JOSEPH VAILL.

NOTE I.

The following petition is taken from the Appendix to Mr. Foot's Historical Discourse on Brookfield, as being peculiarly appropriate to be preserved in connection with a history of the church:

The petition of the inhabitants of Brookfield to the Honored General Court assembled at Boston, November 1698, humbly showeth:—

First, That we seem to be called of God to continue our habitation in this place; we are low in the world, and it would be a breaking thing to our estates to remove to any other plantation. And the land here is very capable of entertaining a considerable body of people; though inhabitants have been slow to come to us by reason of the war, yet the land is very encouraging, capable to afford a comfortable subsistence to many families.

Second, That it is an intolerable burden to continue as we have done, without the preaching of the word. God doth require not only family worship, but his public worship. It is the ordinance of God that, on the Sabbath day, there should be an holy convocation ; and that his word be preached by those who are able and faithful; and our necessities put us upon it earnestly to desire it; both we and our children need the instructions, rebukes and encouragements of the word; the darkness and deadness of our own hearts, together with the many snares that are in the world, are an experimental conviction to us that we need all those helps and advantages that God hath sanctified for our good.

Third, That we are not able at present to maintain the worship of God; we are but *twelve families*, and are not of estate sufficient to give suitable encouragement to a minister; we are willing to do to the outside of our ability; but though as much as can be expected from us, it will not amount to such a sum as a minister may reasonably require for his labor.

Fourth, That if this Honored Court would please to pity us, and grant us some help for a few years, for the maintenance of a godly, able minister, besides the advantage that it may be to these few families that are here, it would be a means of bringing many other inhabitants to us, whereby we shall be so far assisted that we may of ourselves be able to uphold the worship of God, and not be burdensome to others.

Under these considerations we humbly beg, that this Honored Court would exercise compassion to us, and assign some relief to us out of the public treasury, which we shall look upon, not only as a testimony of your zeal for the worship of God, but also of your tender compassion to the souls of those whom God hath made you fathers of: and your petitioners shall pray, &c.

Read November 23, 1698.

In answer to the above petition,—

Ordered that there be *twenty pounds* paid out of the public Treasury of this Province, towards the support of an orthodox minister for one year to commence from the time of the settlement of such minister amongst them.

Sent up to the Honorable the Lieutenant Governor and Council for Concurrence. NATHANIEL BYFIELD, *Speaker*.

SIGNED.

Samuel O. Owen,	Thomas Barnes,	Hervey Gilbert,
Stephen Gennings,	Jno. Woolcott,	James Pettee,
Samuel Davie,	William Barnes,	Thomas Parsons,
Thomas Rich,	Abyan Bartlett,	Daniel Price.
Jon. Clary,	Joseph Marks,	John Pettee.

Read in Council, November 24, 1698, and voted a concurrence with the Representatives.

ISAIAH ADDINGTON, *Secretary*.

NOTE II.

TERMS OF SETTLEMENT AS PROPOSED TO MR. WARD, AND HIS ANSWER OF ACCEPTANCE.

At a legal meeting of the first precinct in the town of Brookfield on Monday the 26th day of August, 1771, the parish passed a vote of concurrence with the church in the choice of Mr. Ephraim Ward of Newton for the minister of the church and congregation in this place. And then,

" *Voted*, That upon the said Mr. Ward becoming the ordained minister of this Church and Congregation, there be given, granted and paid to him the sum of *one hundred and twenty pounds* lawful money of this Province as a *settlement*, to enable him to settle in this place as a minister,—the one half to be paid to him at the end of one year from the day of his ordination, and the other half in two years from said day.

Voted, That upon condition the said Mr. Ward shall become the ordained minister of this Church and Congregration, and upon condition the said Mr. Ward shall not claim any right or interest arising from the ministerial land now sold, that there be given, granted and paid to the said Mr. Ward, the sum of *sixty pounds* as a *salary* for the first year, and the like sum for the second year, at the end of each year; and the sum of *sixty-six pounds, thirteen shillings and four pence* for the third year; and the last mentioned sum every year afterwards, during his carrying on the work of the Gospel ministry in this precinct,—the said salary to commence at the day of his acceptance of this grant and closing with the terms thereof, the money to be computed at the rate of six shillings and eight pence per ounce silver; but to be paid in the then current money of this Province.

Voted, That in case the said Mr. Ward shall, for one year together during his ministry, be rendered unable to perform the publick duty of his office personally, he shall be allowed the *one-half* of the above-granted salary, and no more, during his continuance in the relation of a minister to this people, unless he shall be restored to health, and perform said duty.

Voted, That there be given, granted and delivered to said Mr. Ward at his dwelling-house annually in said precinct *thirty cords of fire-wood* during his continuance in the ministry here, to commence when he shall begin house-keeping, the said wood to be eight feet in length.

Voted, That the foregoing grants and this contract is upon the express condition the said Mr. Ward shall make no claim to any ministerial land in this town, or the incomes arising by the sale thereof; but the same shall be and remain with the people to enable them to pay the salary before granted."

Mr. Ward signified his acceptance of the above terms, September 13th, in the following words:—

" *To Jedidiah Foster Esq., Moderator of a meeting in the first precinct in Brookfield, to be communicated.*

Gentlemen:—After the most mature, deliberate consideration (the time would admit) of the general invitation you have given me to settle among you, and take upon me the pastoral care of the Church and Congregation in this precinct, considering the encouragement you gave as a settlement, and the sum you offer as a salary, although not agreeable to my expectations, and attended with some peculiar restrictions, yet for the sake of the peace of the society, and hoping for the continuance of your friendship and affection, I accept of your proposals, and do hereby signify my closing with the terms thereof. Praying that, by the divine aid and assistance, I may faithfully discharge the important trust when committed to me; wishing that grace, mercy and peace may be multiplied in this place; and that we may long be mutual blessings and comforts to each other in this life, and finally meet and rejoice together in endless happiness,

I remain, Gentlemen, your sincere friend and humble servant,

EPHRAIM WARD.

Brookfield, first precinct, September 13, 1771."

NOTE III.

THE ORIGINAL AND PRESENT COVENANT OF THE CHURCH.

You do now in the presence of the great and holy GOD, the elect Angels, and this assembly of witnesses, enter into a solemn and perpetual covenant, never to be forgotton, never to be broken.

You sincerely and cordially give up yourself to that GOD whose name alone is JEHOVAH; taking GOD the Father to be your GOD and Father, GOD the son to be your only Saviour and Redeemer, GOD the Holy Ghost to be your Sanctifier and Comforter.

You submit yourself to Christ, and accept him as the Prophet, Priest, and King of your soul, the Great Head of the Church, and the only Mediator of the covenant of grace; promising that by the assistance of the Holy Spirit you will keep the covenant of the Lord inviolably; that you will cleave to the Lord Jesus Christ by faith and Gospel obedience;—and will endeavor to reform your life as to all known sin, whether open or secret; —will live in the conscientious discharge of all duty toward GOD and man;—walking in all the commandments and ordinances of the Lord blamelessly;—that you will endeavor that the inward temper of your mind be conformed to GOD's will and word;—and that you will follow the excellent example which Christ has set you for the rule of your life.

You also give up yourself to this Church in the Lord; and freely covenant and bind yourself to walk as a regular member of Christ's church; to obey them that have rule over you in the Lord—to read GOD's word, and to live in the practice of *social and secret* prayer, and in diligent attendance on the word preached, and ordinances administered: and relying on the grace and all-sufficiency of Christ, which are sufficient for you—You promise to walk according to what you now know, or shall know to be your duty.

Do you sincerely and cordially consent to the covenant now proposed?

We then receive you as a sincere disciple of Christ and a member of the same church with ourselves, promising, so long as GOD shall continue you among us, to watch over you with meekness and brotherly love; and may the Lord add to the numbers and graces of his church, and finally bring us all to join the general Assembly, and Church of the First-born, whose names are written in heaven. AMEN.

NOTE IV.

The number of members of which the church was composed when Mr. Ward's ministry *commenced*, in 1771, is not ascertained. We gather from the Catalogue about *ninety* names. But as the record of admissions begins only fourteen years earlier, (in 1758), many names are undoubtedly lost.

The following TABLE, carefully compiled by Mr. Cordley (former pastor) from the Catalogue prepared by himself, and continued by the present pastor, indicates the annual increase or decrease in the membership of the Church during each pastorate for the last half century, beginning with the year 1816.

Mr. Phelps was settled October 23, 1816.

Year.	Month.	Additions.	Removals.	Members.
1816	October 23,			236
1817	January 1,	4	4	236
1818	January 1,	13	11	238
1819	January 1,	57	6	289
1820	January 1,	65	14	340
1821	January 1,	8	9	339
1822	January 1,	10	10	339
1823	January 1,		6	333
1824	January 1,	2	13	322
1825	January 1,	2	12	312
1826	January 1,	4	13	303
1826	October 25,	3	16	290

Mr. Phelps was dismissed October 25, 1826.

Mr. Foot was settled October 25, 1826.

Year.	Month.	Additions.	Removals.	Members.
1827	January 1,	1	1	290
1828	January 1,	84	13	361
1829	January 1,	13	8	366
1830	January 1,	7	9	364
1831	January 1,	11	16	359
1832	January 1,	5	19	345
1832	May 1,	1	4	342

Mr. Foot was dismissed May 1, 1832.

Mr. Horton was settled August 15, 1832.

Year.	Month.	Additions.	Removals.	Members.
1832	August 15,		4	338
1833	Jauuary 1,	10	12	336
1834	January 1,	11	24	323
1835	January 1,	8	21	310
1836	January 1,	99	28	381
1837	January 1,	6	12	375
1838	January 1,	11	19	367
1839	January 1,	2	18	351
1840	January 1,	29	21	359
1841	January 1,	3	14	348
1841	September 15,	11	14	345

Mr. Horton was dismissed September 15, 1841.

Year.	Month.	Additions.	Removals.	Members.
1842	January 1,	1	6	340
1842	January 12,			340

Mr. Chase was settled January 12, 1842.

Year.	Month.	Additions.	Removals.	Members.
1843	January 1,	13	22	331
1843	October 27,	2	15	318

Mr. Chase was dismissed October 27, 1843.

Year.	Month.	Additions.	Removals.	Members.
1844	January 1,		5	313
1844	December 19,	3	14	302

Mr. Parker was settled December 19, 1844.

Year.	Month.	Additions.	Removals.	Members.
1845	January 1,	1	1	302
1846	January 1,	15	14	303
1847	January 1,	12	16	299
1848	January 1,	6	16	289
1849	January 1,	21	13	297
1850	January 1,	2	16	283
1851	January 1,	7	10	280
1851	April 7,	4	3	281

Mr. Parker was dismissed April 7, 1851.

Year.	Month.	Additions.	Removals.	Members.
1852	January 1,		12	269
1852	November 17,	6	11	264

Mr. Byington was settled November 17, 1852.

Year.	Month.	Additions.	Removals.	Members.
1853	January 1,	1	2	263
1854	January 1,	14	10	267
1855	January 1,	18	12	273
1856	January 1,	7	22	258
1857	January 1,	3	13	248
1858	January 1,	8	16	240
1858	October 28,	19	18	241

Mr. Byington was dismissed October 28, 1858.

Year.	Month.	Additions.	Removals.	Members.
1859	January 1,		2	239
1859	June 28,	3	5	237

Mr. Cordley was settled June 28, 1859.

Year.	Month.	Additions.	Removals.	Members.
1860	January 1,	15	5	247
1861	January 1,	9	18	238
1862	January 1,	11	11	238
1862	June 23,	3	7	234

Mr. Cordley was dismissed June 23, 1862.

Year.	Month.	Additions.	Removals.	Members.
1863	January 1,	2	1	235
1864	January 1,	0	6	229
1864	October 4,	1	39*	191

Mr. Dunham was settled October 4, 1864.

Year.	Month.	Additions.	Removals.	Members.
1865	January 1,	27	0	218
1866	January 1,	20	7	231
1867	January 1,	10	10	231
1867	December 1,	78	9	300

The lithographic likeness of Rev. Mr. Ward accompanying this pamphlet, has been kindly furnished at considerable expense by his grandson, George L. Ward, Esq., of Cambridge.

* Of these *twenty-four* were *stricken from the roll*, having been absent many years without taking letters of dismission and recommendation to other churches.

www.ingramcontent.com/pod-product-compliance
Lightning Source LLC
LaVergne TN
LVHW021421110826
845150LV00007B/2020

* 9 7 8 1 4 2 5 5 0 8 6 3 0 *